LETTERS TO TEENAGERS

LESSONS ON BUILDING A GREAT LIFE

DR. ASHISH GUPTA

Made with ♥ on the Notion Press Platform
www.notionpress.com

To every teenager who has ever felt lost, unsure, or overwhelmed by life's challenges—**this book is for you.**

To those who dare to dream big but sometimes doubt themselves—**may this book remind you of your strength and potential.**

To the parents, teachers, and mentors who guide young minds—**your support shapes the future.**

And to my younger self—**I wish you had this book when you needed it most.**

With hope, belief, and endless encouragement

Contents

Contents

Contents

A Letter To You, Dear Teenager

Dear Teenager,

As you hold this book in your hands, I want you to know that it is not just a collection of words—it's a conversation between you and me—a conversation about **life, success, failures, dreams, fears, and everything in between. It's a guide, a friend, and a mentor rolled into one.**

I know being a teenager isn't easy. You are at a stage where you are expected to grow up, make decisions, and figure out who you are, all while dealing with the **chaos of school, friendships, family, and an ever-changing world.** It can feel overwhelming at times, and that's okay.

But here's the truth: **your teenage years are the foundation of the rest of your life.** The choices you make now, the habits you build, and the lessons you learn will shape your future. That's why I wrote this book—to share with you the wisdom that can become your guiding light.

Through these letters, I will talk to you about things that truly matter—how to build confidence, handle failures, choose the right friends, develop strong values, and create a life of meaning. These are not just lessons from textbooks but insights from real-life experiences—mine and of many great people who have walked this path before you.

You don't have to figure everything out right now, but I want you to remember this:

You are capable of great things.
You are stronger than your struggles.
You have the power to create the life you dream of.

This book is here to help you see that. Read it like a conversation with an older friend who genuinely wants to see you win in life. Read it with an open heart, reflect on the lessons, and most importantly—apply them.

Your journey is just beginning, and I promise, it's going to be incredible.

With belief in you,
AG

Why This Book?

Dear Teenager,

Life doesn't come with a manual, but if it did, I wish it included the lessons I am about to share with you in this book.

The teenage years are a confusing mix of excitement and uncertainty. It's a time when you are expected to dream big, yet society often tells you to play it safe. You are encouraged to be independent, yet you are constantly reminded to follow the rules. You want to stand out, yet fitting in feels just as important. In the middle of all this, **how do you figure out what really matters?**

That's exactly why I wrote this book—for **you.**

You don't need more people telling you what to do with your life. You need someone who understands what you're going through and can give you **real, practical, and timeless wisdom**—the kind that will help you navigate the challenges ahead and build a life that you truly love.

This book isn't about memorizing facts, scoring top marks, or following a strict formula for success. Instead, it's about understanding the deeper principles that shape **who you become**—your mindset, your habits, your choices, and your values.

Inside these pages, you will find lessons on **confidence, failure, success, relationships, money, mindset, and**

purpose—all written in the form of letters just for you. These are the things I wish someone had told me when I was your age. Things that could have saved me from unnecessary struggles and helped me make better decisions.

I don't claim to have all the answers, but I do know this:

- If you take charge of your life today, your future will be incredible.
- If you develop the right habits now, success will come naturally to you.
- If you learn how to handle setbacks, nothing will stop you from achieving greatness.

You have so much potential inside you, and my only goal is to help you see it for yourself.

This book is **your guide, your mentor, and your friend**. Read it with an open mind, reflect on the lessons, and apply them in your life. **Your future self will thank you for it.**

Are you ready? Let's begin.

With belief in you,
AG

The Power Of Wisdom In Your Hands

Dear Teenager,

Imagine if you had a superpower—one that could help you make better decisions, overcome any challenge, and create a life filled with success, happiness, and purpose. **That superpower exists. It's called wisdom.**

Wisdom isn't about knowing everything. It's about understanding life deeply and making choices that lead to the best outcomes. It's what separates people who keep repeating the same mistakes from those who grow and thrive. **And the best part? Wisdom isn't something you are born with—it's something you can develop.**

In your hands, you hold more than just a book. You hold ideas, insights, and life lessons that have been passed down through generations, tested by time, and lived by some of the world's most successful and fulfilled people. The pages you are about to read contain **wisdom that can change your life—if you let it.**

Many people spend their entire lives chasing success, happiness, or money, but they never stop to seek wisdom. Without wisdom:

- People make the same mistakes over and over.
- They fall into traps of negativity, fear, and bad habits.
- They feel lost, even when they seem to have everything.

But with wisdom:

- You can make smarter choices that bring long-term success.
- You learn to handle failures without giving up.
- You build strong relationships and surround yourself with the right people.
- You develop a mindset that helps you grow and achieve your goals.

Wisdom is like a compass—it helps you find your way, even when life gets confusing. And in this fast-changing world, where distractions are endless and bad advice is everywhere, wisdom is more important than ever.

How to Use This Book

The lessons in this book are simple, but their impact can be powerful. However, just reading them isn't enough. **Wisdom only works when you apply it.**

So, here's my advice as you go through this book:

1. **Read with an open mind** – Be willing to challenge the way you think.
2. **Reflect on each lesson** – Ask yourself, "How does this apply to my life?"
3. **Take action** – Small changes today will shape a great future.
4. **Come back to these lessons often** – Wisdom grows deeper with time.

Every page of this book has one goal—to help you become the best version of yourself. The power of wisdom is now in your hands. What you do with it is up to you.

With great hope for your future,
AG

About The Author

Dr. Ashish Gupta is an education leader, career coach, and entrepreneur dedicated to empowering the next generation of students and professionals. With over 14 years of experience in higher education, he has worked with some of India's top universities, shaping the future of admissions, outreach, and student success.

Dr. Ashish has mentored thousands of students, helping

them make informed career decisions, develop essential skills, and prepare for a rapidly evolving world. His mission is to create one million future-ready students in India, equipping them with the knowledge and tools to build meaningful and successful careers.

Beyond education, Dr. Ashish is a thought leader in personal development, leadership, and Indic wisdom, drawing insights from ancient Indian scriptures and modern-day success strategies. He has authored multiple books covering topics such as leadership, personal growth, career success, and entrepreneurship, always with a focus on bringing Indian wisdom into modern learning.

"Letters to Teenagers: Lessons on Building a Great Life" is a reflection of his deep commitment to guiding young minds. This book shares practical wisdom, real-life lessons, and actionable strategies to help teenagers navigate life with confidence, purpose, and resilience.

When he's not coaching students or writing books, Dr. Ashish enjoys exploring India's rich cultural heritage, engaging in thought-provoking discussions, and continuously learning from the world around him.

Connect with Dr. Ashish Gupta:
LinkedIn: https://www.linkedin.com/in/theashishgupta/
Website: ashishgupta.co.in

Part 1: The Foundation of a Great Life

CHAPTER I

The Most Important Decision: Who You Become

Dear Teenager,

If there is one decision that will shape your entire life, it is **who you choose to become.**

Not what job you'll have.
Not how much money you'll make.
Not where you'll live.

All of those things matter, but they are **outcomes** of a much bigger decision—the decision to define who you are, what you stand for, and the kind of person you will be.

You Are Not Just a Product of Circumstances: Some people believe that life just "happens" to them. They think their future depends on where they are born, their family background, or pure luck. **But the truth is, your life is shaped by your choices.**

Yes, circumstances can make things easier or harder, but **who you become is always in your hands.** You get to decide whether you will be disciplined or lazy, kind or selfish, courageous or fearful. These decisions will ultimately determine the quality of your life far more than any external factor.

Your Identity is a Choice

Ask yourself:

- **What kind of person do I want to be?**
- **What values do I want to live by?**
- **How do I want people to remember me?**

Most people never ask themselves these questions. They drift through life, influenced by trends, peer pressure, and social media, without ever defining who they truly want to be. And as a result, they live a life shaped by others instead of taking control.

But you are different. **You are reading this book because you want more out of life.**

Building the Best Version of You: Who you become is built by your daily choices and habits. You don't become successful overnight, just like you don't become a failure overnight. It's all about the small things you do every day.

Here are some choices that will shape your future:

- **Choosing discipline over laziness** – The small habits you build today will create your future.
- **Choosing growth over comfort** – Challenges and struggles will make you stronger.
- **Choosing responsibility over excuses** – You are the driver of your life, not a passenger.
- **Choosing kindness over selfishness** – The way you treat people will define your relationships.

- **Choosing learning over ignorance** – Every book you read, every skill you learn, and every lesson you apply will make you wiser.

Your Future is in Your Hands: Right now, you are at a stage where life is full of possibilities. You can become **anyone** you want to be. The real question is: **Are you willing to make the right choices to become the best version of yourself?**

No one can answer that question for you. But I hope you make the choice to invest in yourself, to grow, to become strong, wise, and kind. Because that will be **the most important decision of your life.**

With belief in you,
AG

CHAPTER II

The Power of Character: Honesty, Integrity & Discipline

Dear Teenager,

In a world obsessed with success, fame, and external achievements, it's easy to forget what truly defines a person: **character.**

Your character is who you are when no one is watching. It's the foundation of your life, the invisible force that determines your relationships, your reputation, and ultimately, your success. You can be smart, talented, and hardworking, but without strong character, none of it will matter in the long run.

Why Character Matters More Than Success: Look around, and you'll see countless examples of talented people who ruined their lives because they lacked strong character—athletes caught cheating, politicians involved in corruption, business leaders who lost everything because of greed.

On the other hand, history is also full of people who built great legacies because of their **honesty, integrity, and discipline.** These are the people who are respected, admired, and remembered—not just for what they achieved, but for who they were.

You get to decide which side you want to be on.

The Three Pillars of Strong Character

1. Honesty – The Courage to Tell the Truth

Being honest isn't always easy. Sometimes, lying seems like the easier way out. But the truth has a way of catching up, and once you lose someone's trust, it's almost impossible to earn it back.

Honesty isn't just about not lying—it's about being truthful to yourself.

- Be honest about your strengths and weaknesses.
- Be honest in your relationships.
- Be honest in your work and studies.

A person who is known for their honesty is trusted, and trust is the foundation of all success.

2. Integrity – Doing the Right Thing, Even When No One is Watching

Integrity is about standing by your values, even when it's difficult. It's easy to be good when people are watching, but what truly matters is what you do when no one is around.

Integrity means:

- Keeping your promises, even when it's inconvenient.

- Standing up for what is right, even if you are standing alone.
- Refusing to cheat, lie, or take shortcuts, even when no one will find out.

A person with integrity doesn't need to prove anything—**their actions speak for themselves.**

3. Discipline – The Strength to Do What Needs to Be Done

Discipline is the bridge between who you are today and who you want to become. Talent and intelligence mean nothing if you don't have the discipline to work hard and stay consistent.

Discipline means:

- Waking up on time, even when you don't feel like it.
- Studying and working hard, even when distractions are everywhere.
- Controlling your emotions and actions, instead of letting them control you.

Most people fail not because they lack talent, but because they lack **discipline.** If you learn to control your mind, you can control your future.

Your Character is Your Destiny: Your character is your greatest asset. It will define your relationships, your opportunities, and your legacy. The world respects people with strong character because they are rare.

So ask yourself:

- Am I honest, even when it's hard?
- Do I have integrity, even when no one is watching?
- Am I disciplined, even when I don't feel like it?

If the answer is yes, you are on the path to greatness. If not, the good news is **you can start building your character today.**

Because in the end, success may come and go, **but your character stays with you forever.**

With belief in you,
AG

CHAPTER III

Why Hard Work Beats Talent

Dear Teenager,

You've probably heard people say, **"That person is so talented!"** when talking about a great athlete, a brilliant student, or a successful entrepreneur. Talent is often seen as something magical—either you have it, or you don't. But let me tell you a truth that will change the way you see success:

Hard work beats talent when talent doesn't work hard.

Yes, talent is great. It can give you a head start. But in the long run, the people who win in life are not always the most talented—they are the ones who work the hardest.

The Illusion of Talent: Many people believe that successful individuals were "born with it." But when you dig deeper, you'll realize that behind every great achievement is years of dedication, sacrifice, and persistence.

Think about:

- Sachin Tendulkar – He wasn't born a cricket legend; he practiced tirelessly every single day.
- Virat Kohli – His fitness, discipline, and work ethic turned him into one of the world's best cricketers.
- A.P.J. Abdul Kalam – He came from a humble background but worked relentlessly to become India's

most loved scientist and president.

They were not just talented. They were obsessed with hard work.

Why Hard Work is the Ultimate Superpower

1. Hard Work Creates Skill: Talent can only take you so far. Real skill is developed through hours, days, and years of effort. The best musicians, writers, athletes, and entrepreneurs didn't rely on natural talent alone—they mastered their craft by working harder than anyone else.
2. Hard Work Builds Discipline & Grit: Life is not easy. Challenges will come. If you rely only on talent, the moment things get tough, you will give up. But if you are used to working hard, you will have the discipline and mental strength to push through obstacles.
3. Hard Work Attracts Opportunities: People recognize hard workers. Teachers, mentors, and employers always support those who are willing to go the extra mile. The harder you work, the more doors open for you.
4. Hard Work Beats People Who Are Lazy With Their Talent: The world is full of talented people who never did anything great because they didn't put in the effort. But history belongs to those who put in the hours, sweat, and struggle.

Talent vs. Hard Work: A Simple Truth

- A talented student who doesn't study will fail.

- A naturally athletic person who doesn't train will lose.
- A gifted singer who doesn't practice will fade away.

But a hardworking student, athlete, or singer will always keep improving—and improvement leads to success.

How to Develop a Hard-Working Mindset

- Show up every day – Talent doesn't matter if you're inconsistent. Put in the work, no matter how small.
- Push yourself beyond comfort – Growth happens when you challenge yourself.
- Learn from failure – Hard workers see failures as lessons, not as reasons to quit.
- Outwork everyone around you – Make effort your competitive advantage.
- Stay patient – Hard work compounds over time. Keep going, and results will follow.

The Choice is Yours

You can either believe that success is only for the "talented," or you can choose to work hard and make success inevitable.

Talent might give you a head start, but hard work will always take you further.

So, what's your choice?

With belief in you,

AG

13

CHAPTER IV

The Magic of a Growth Mindset

Dear Teenager,

What if I told you that your intelligence, skills, and abilities are not fixed—that you have the power to improve at anything you set your mind to?

Many people believe that their abilities are limited. They think they are "bad at math," "not creative," or "not smart enough"—as if their potential was set in stone. But the truth is, your brain is like a muscle—the more you use it, the stronger it gets.

This is the power of a growth mindset—the belief that you can improve, grow, and develop through effort, learning, and perseverance.

Growth Mindset vs. Fixed Mindset: Your mindset shapes how you see challenges, failures, and success. Let's look at the difference between a fixed mindset and a growth mindset:

Fixed Mindset	Growth Mindset
"I'm either good at this or I'm not."	"I can improve if I work hard."
"I failed, so I'm not good enough."	"I failed, so I need to try a different approach."
"I don't like challenges."	"Challenges help me grow."
"I'm not a math person."	"I can get better at math with practice."
"I don't want to look stupid."	"I'd rather learn than worry about what others think."

Growth Mindset vs. Fixed Mindset

Why a Growth Mindset is a Superpower

1. You Learn Faster – When you believe you can improve, you put in more effort, and effort leads to results.
2. You Don't Fear Failure – Failure becomes a lesson, not a reason to quit.
3. You Stay Motivated – Instead of giving up, you focus on progress.
4. You Achieve More – Many of the world's most successful people got there because they kept learning and improving.

Real-Life Examples of a Growth Mindset

- Michael Jordan was cut from his high school basketball team. Instead of quitting, he trained harder and became one of the greatest players of all time.
- Thomas Edison failed thousands of times before inventing the light bulb. He said, "I have not failed. I've just found 10,000 ways that won't work."
- J.K. Rowling was rejected by 12 publishers before Harry Potter became a global phenomenon.

None of these people were "born successful." They developed their abilities through hard work and persistence.

How to Build a Growth Mindset

- Embrace Challenges – See difficulties as opportunities to grow.
- Replace "I can't" with "I can learn" – Your abilities are not fixed.
- Celebrate Effort, Not Just Results – Hard work is more important than instant success.
- Learn from Mistakes – Failure is part of the learning process.
- Surround Yourself with Growth-Minded People – Stay around people who encourage learning and growth.

Your Potential is Unlimited

Right now, you might not be the best at everything—but that doesn't mean you never will be. The only limit is how much effort you are willing to put in.

Your brain, your skills, your intelligence—they all grow when you work on them. So, decide today that you will always keep learning, improving, and pushing yourself beyond what you think is possible.

Because the magic of a growth mindset can take you anywhere.

With belief in you,
AG

CHAPTER V

How to Build Self-Confidence That Lasts

Dear Teenager,

Imagine walking into a room full of people and feeling **completely comfortable in your own skin.** Imagine facing challenges with the unshakable belief that you can handle anything life throws at you. **That's confidence.** And the good news? **Confidence is not something you are born with—it's something you build.**

Many people think confidence comes from being naturally gifted, looking a certain way, or being good at everything. But that's not true. **Real confidence comes from within**—from how you see yourself, how you handle failures, and how you show up in life.

Why Confidence Matters

- **Confident people take action.** They don't sit on the sidelines waiting for permission to succeed.
- **Confidence attracts opportunities.** When you believe in yourself, others believe in you too.
- **Confidence helps you handle criticism.** You don't break down when someone doubts you.
- **Confidence leads to success.** Most successful people weren't born confident—they became confident by pushing through challenges.

The Truth About Confidence: Confidence is not about being the loudest person in the room. It's not about never feeling nervous. **Confidence is about trusting yourself, even when things are uncertain.**

So, how do you build confidence that lasts?

1. Keep Promises to Yourself: If you say you will do something—do it. When you keep breaking promises to yourself (like saying you'll wake up early but hitting snooze instead), you start doubting your own abilities. But when you follow through, even on small things, your confidence grows.

Start small: If you promise yourself you'll read for 10 minutes daily, do it. If you say you'll work out, show up. Keeping commitments builds self-trust, which fuels confidence.

2. Focus on Progress, Not Perfection: Many people feel insecure because they think they're not "good enough." But confidence isn't about being perfect—it's about improving.

Instead of saying, "I'm bad at math," say, "I'm improving in math."
Instead of thinking, "I can't speak in public," remind yourself, "I can get better with practice."

Growth leads to confidence. The more you improve, the more you believe in yourself.

3. Step Out of Your Comfort Zone Daily: Confidence

doesn't come from staying comfortable—it comes from doing things that scare you. Every time you push past fear, your confidence grows.

Start a conversation with a new person.
Raise your hand in class.
Try something you've never done before.

Each small victory adds up, and over time, you become unshakable.

4. Improve Your Body Language: Your posture, facial expressions, and voice affect how confident you feel.

Stand tall. Slouching makes you feel and look unsure of yourself.
Make eye contact. It shows you're engaged and self-assured.
Speak clearly and with energy. Confident people don't mumble or rush their words.

Your body affects your mind. Act confident, and you'll start feeling confident.

5. Stop Comparing Yourself to Others: The fastest way to kill confidence is by constantly measuring yourself against others. **Your only competition is YOU.**

Instead of focusing on how successful someone else is, focus on **how much YOU have improved.**
Social media makes people look perfect, but remember—people only show their highlights, not their struggles.

Stay in your lane and focus on your own journey.

6. Develop Real Skills: Confidence is not just about "feeling good"—it's about actually being good at something.

Learn a skill. (Public speaking, writing, coding, a sport—anything!)
Work hard to get better at it.
The better you become at something, the more confidence you naturally feel.

When you have real skills, you don't need to "fake" confidence—it comes automatically.

7. Handle Failures Like a Winner: Confident people fail just as much as others—but they don't let it destroy them. Instead, they see failure as a learning experience.

If you fail a test, study harder and try again.
If you get rejected, don't take it personally—use it as motivation.
If something goes wrong, ask, "What can I learn from this?"

Every time you bounce back, your confidence becomes stronger.

8. Surround Yourself with Positive People: Confidence grows when you are around people who uplift you, not those who tear you down.

Spend time with people who encourage and inspire you.
Avoid toxic friends who make you feel small or insecure.

The right environment can make all the difference in how you see yourself.

9. Accept Yourself as You Are: True confidence isn't about proving yourself to others—it's about being comfortable with who you are.

Stop waiting for approval from others.
Own your strengths AND your flaws.
Be proud of yourself, even if you're still a work in progress.

Confidence is built by embracing yourself completely.

Confidence is a Choice: You don't wake up one day magically confident. **You build it, step by step, through your actions, mindset, and habits.**

Starting today, choose to:

- Keep promises to yourself.
- Step out of your comfort zone.
- Stop comparing yourself to others.
- Learn, grow, and take action.

Because confidence isn't something you are born with—it's something you create. **And you have the power to create it.**

With belief in you,
AG

CHAPTER VI

Failures Are Not the End, They Are the Beginning

Dear Teenager,

Have you ever failed at something and felt like giving up? Maybe you didn't get the marks you wanted, didn't make the team, or felt embarrassed after making a mistake. I know how that feels. **Failure can be painful. It can shake your confidence. It can make you question yourself.**

But here's the truth that most people don't realize:
Failure is not the end. It is the beginning of success.

The Myth About Failure: Many people think failure means they are not good enough. But the reality is:

- Failure is **not a sign of weakness**—it's a sign that you are trying.
- Failure **does not define you**—what you do after failure does.
- Failure **isn't permanent**—it's just a step toward success.

In fact, failure is one of the best teachers in life. Some of the most successful people in the world **failed more times than they succeeded**, but they kept going.

Great People Who Turned Failure into Success

- Michael Jordan – Cut from his high school basketball team but kept practicing until he became the greatest player in NBA history.
- Albert Einstein – His teachers thought he was slow, but he went on to change the world of science.
- J.K. Rowling – Rejected by 12 publishers before Harry Potter became a global phenomenon.
- Steve Jobs – Fired from his own company (Apple) but came back to build one of the most successful companies in the world.

None of them would have achieved greatness if they had given up after failing.

Why Failure is a Good Thing

1. **Failure Helps You Learn Faster:** Every time you fail, you learn what doesn't work. Each mistake teaches you something new. The faster you fail, the faster you learn, and the faster you succeed.
2. **Failure Builds Mental Strength:** Every time you rise after failing, you become mentally stronger. Success is not about never falling—it's about getting up every time you do.
3. **Failure Means You Are Taking Action:** The only way to never fail is to never try anything new—and that's a guaranteed way to stay stuck in life. If you are failing, it means you are pushing your limits and growing.
4. **Failure Makes Success More Meaningful:** If success came easy, it wouldn't feel special. The struggles you go through make the victory sweeter.

How to Handle Failure Like a Winner

- Accept It – Instead of denying or feeling ashamed, accept failure as part of the journey.
- Analyze It – Ask yourself: What went wrong? What can I do differently next time?
- Adjust & Improve – Change your approach, learn from mistakes, and try again.
- Stay Positive – Don't let failure make you feel like a failure. Separate your results from your self-worth.
- Keep Going – The only real failure is quitting. If you keep trying, you are never truly failing.

A New Way to See Failure

From now on, every time you fail, **don't say, "I failed." Say, "I learned."**

- Failed a test? You learned what to study better.
- Lost a competition? You learned how to improve your skills.
- Made a mistake? You learned what not to do next time.

The Choice is Yours
When failure happens, you have two choices:

1. **Let it defeat you** and stop trying.
2. **Use it as fuel** to work harder, get smarter, and come back stronger.

Winners choose the second option. **Be a winner.**

Because failure is not the end—it is just the beginning of something greater.

With belief in you,
AG

CHAPTER VII

Why Reading Can Change Your Life

Dear Teenager,

If I told you that there's a single habit that can make you smarter, more successful, and more confident, would you be interested? What if I told you that this habit has transformed the lives of the world's greatest leaders, entrepreneurs, and thinkers?

That habit is **reading.**

Books are like secret conversations with the world's smartest minds. When you read, you get direct access to the wisdom of people who have lived before you, struggled before you, and succeeded before you. You don't need to figure everything out on your own—books allow you to learn from others' experiences and mistakes.

How Reading Transforms Your Life

1. **Reading Makes You Smarter:** Your brain is like a muscle—the more you use it, the stronger it gets. Every book you read expands your mind, improves your thinking, and gives you new ideas. **Reading is the fastest way to learn anything.**

- Want to be better at business? Read books by successful entrepreneurs.

- Want to be more confident? Read books on personal development.
- Want to be a great leader? Read about great leaders from history.

Everything you need to learn is already written somewhere—you just need to find the right book.

2. **Reading Helps You See the World Differently:** Books take you beyond your surroundings and introduce you to new perspectives. They allow you to see the world through the eyes of people from different cultures, different times, and different experiences.

The more you read, the more open-minded and understanding you become. **Books make you wiser.**

3. Reading Gives You a Competitive Advantage: Most people stop learning after school. But those who keep reading and learning stay ahead in life. If you read just **one book a month,** in five years, you will have read **60 books**—which is more than most people read in their entire lifetime!

Imagine the advantage you will have over others if you develop this habit now.

4. Reading Improves Focus and Mental Clarity: In today's world of distractions—social media, video games, and endless scrolling—**your ability to focus is your superpower.** Reading trains your brain to concentrate for long periods, helping you in school, work, and life.

5. Reading Helps You Communicate Better: Great communicators are great readers. The more you read, the more words you learn, and the better you express yourself. Whether in conversations, writing, or public speaking, **reading improves your ability to communicate with confidence.**

6. Reading Reduces Stress and Makes You Happier: A good book can take you to another world, give you hope, and inspire you. When you read, your mind calms down, your stress decreases, and your imagination comes alive.

What Should You Read?

You don't have to start with boring textbooks. Read what excites you!

- Biographies of great people
- Books on self-improvement
- Business & money books
- Fiction that expands your creativity
- Books on history, science, and philosophy

How to Build a Reading Habit

- Start small – Read 10 pages a day. Over time, increase your reading time.
- Always carry a book – Keep a book with you when traveling or waiting somewhere.
- Replace social media with books – Spend 15-30 minutes reading instead of scrolling.

- Take notes – Highlight important lessons and apply them in life.
- Join a reading challenge – Set a goal to read a certain number of books per year.

The Choice is Yours

You can either let social media and entertainment control your mind, or you can feed your mind with knowledge and wisdom.

Every book you read makes you a better, smarter, and stronger person.

So, what will you start reading today?

With belief in you,
AG

CHAPTER VIII

The People You Surround Yourself With Shape You

Dear Teenager,

Have you ever noticed how your mood, habits, and even the way you think change depending on the **people you spend time with?** That's because the people around you shape who you become.

There's a famous saying:
"You are the average of the five people you spend the most time with."

Think about that for a moment. The people you hang out with influence:

- Your mindset
- Your habits
- Your level of confidence
- Your ambition and goals

So, if you surround yourself with **driven, positive, and hardworking people,** you will naturally adopt their mindset and habits. But if you spend time with **negative, lazy, or unmotivated people,** they will pull you down without you even realizing it.

Why Your Circle Matters

1. **Your Friends Influence Your Thinking:** If you are around people who constantly complain, gossip, or make excuses, you will start doing the same. But if you surround yourself with people who talk about ideas, solutions, and self-improvement, your thinking will change for the better.

2. Your Circle Affects Your Confidence

- Do your friends encourage you or bring you down?
- Do they support your dreams or make fun of them?
- Do they push you to grow or make you feel small?

3. Being around supportive, ambitious people will help you believe in yourself and push you to do better.

4. You Pick Up the Habits of Those Around You

- If your friends are always wasting time, chances are, you'll do the same.
- If they are focused on learning and growth, you will naturally improve too.
- If they have bad habits, they will eventually influence you.

5. **Habits are contagious. Choose your environment wisely.**

How to Choose the Right People

Ask yourself these questions:

- **Do they inspire me to be better?**
- **Do they support my growth and goals?**
- **Are they honest and trustworthy?**
- **Do I feel positive and energized around them?**

If the answer is **yes,** they are the right people for you.

If the answer is **no,** it may be time to **distance yourself from those who hold you back** and seek out people who lift you up.

What If You're Surrounded by the Wrong People?

- **Limit your time with negative influences.** You don't have to cut them off completely, but spend less time with them.
- **Look for mentors and role models.** Learn from people who inspire you, even if they are not in your immediate circle.
- **Find communities that align with your values.** Join clubs, groups, or online communities where people share your interests and ambitions.
- **Be the positive influence.** If your friends are stuck in negative habits, be the one to introduce growth, learning, and ambition into your group.

Your Environment is Your Future

If you want to become great, **surround yourself with**

greatness.

If you want to succeed, **be around people who push you forward, not pull you back.**

So, take a moment today and ask yourself: **Are the people around me shaping me into the person I want to be?**

If not, it's time to make a change. Because **your circle will either elevate you or limit you. Choose wisely.**

With belief in you,
AG

Part 2: Mastering Your Mind & Emotions

CHAPTER IX

Understanding Your Own Thoughts & Feelings

Dear Teenager,

Have you ever felt overwhelmed by your thoughts or emotions, unsure of why you feel the way you do? Maybe you've had days where your mind is racing with worries, or moments where you feel frustrated but don't know why.

You are not alone. **Every person goes through this.** But here's the secret: **the better you understand your own thoughts and feelings, the better control you have over your life.**

Why Understanding Yourself is Important: Most people go through life reacting to their emotions without questioning them. They feel sad but don't know why. They get angry without understanding the real reason. They feel anxious but never stop to explore what's triggering it.

But when you start to understand your own thoughts and feelings, you gain power over them. Instead of being controlled by emotions, you learn how to **manage them, work through them, and use them to grow.**

Your Thoughts Shape Your Life

The way you think determines:

- How you see yourself
- How you handle challenges
- How you treat others
- What kind of future will you create

Your thoughts become your beliefs, and your beliefs shape your actions. **If you think you are not good enough, you will act like it. If you believe you can improve, you will work towards it.**

How to Become More Aware of Your Thoughts

1. **Pause & Observe** – Instead of reacting immediately, take a moment to ask yourself: What am I thinking? Why am I thinking this way?
2. **Challenge Negative Thoughts** – If you catch yourself thinking "I'll never be good at this," stop and ask, "Is that really true? Or can I improve?"
3. **Write It Down** – Keeping a journal of your thoughts and feelings helps you process them better.
4. **Focus on Solutions** – If you find yourself stuck in negative thinking, shift your focus to: "What can I do about this?"

Understanding Your Feelings

Your emotions are not random. They are signals trying to tell you something.

- **Anger** – Often a sign that something is unfair or that your boundaries are being crossed.

- **Sadness** – Can mean you need to process a loss or disappointment.
- **Anxiety** – A sign that something feels uncertain or that you need to prepare better.
- **Happiness** – Tells you what truly matters to you.

How to Manage Your Emotions

Acknowledge Them – Instead of ignoring or suppressing feelings, recognize them. It's okay to feel.

Ask "Why?" – Get curious about your emotions. What triggered them?

Express Them in a Healthy Way – Talk to someone, write it down, or channel it into creativity or exercise.

Don't Let Feelings Control You – You have emotions, but you are not your emotions. Learn to pause before reacting.

You Are in Control

The more you understand your own thoughts and feelings, the more power you have over your life.

Most people let their emotions control them. **But you can choose to understand them, work through them, and use them as tools for growth.**

So next time you feel something deeply, instead of ignoring it, **pause and ask: What is this feeling trying to teach me?**

Because when you understand yourself, you gain the power to shape your future.

With belief in you,
AG

CHAPTER X

The Art of Controlling Your Anger & Emotions

Dear Teenager,

Have you ever felt so angry that you said or did something you later regretted? Or maybe you've been overwhelmed by emotions—sadness, frustration, jealousy, or disappointment—without knowing how to handle them.

Emotions are powerful. They can make you feel on top of the world or completely out of control. But here's the truth: **You don't have to be controlled by your emotions—you can learn to control them.**

Why Controlling Your Emotions Matters

Your ability to manage your emotions affects:

- Your relationships with family, friends, and teachers
- Your ability to make good decisions
- Your mental peace and happiness
- Your success in school, work, and life

Many people let their emotions **control them,** leading to impulsive actions, broken relationships, and regrets. But successful, happy people **learn to master their emotions,** using them as a tool for growth instead of destruction.

Understanding Anger: The Most Destructive Emotion

Anger is a normal emotion, but if you don't control it, it can lead to:

- Saying hurtful words that damage relationships
- Making rash decisions that you later regret
- Feeling stressed, anxious, and overwhelmed

The problem isn't **feeling** angry—it's **how you react to it.**

How to Control Your Anger

- **Pause Before Reacting** – When you feel anger rising, take a deep breath. Count to 10 before speaking or acting. This stops you from saying something you'll regret.
- **Identify the Real Reason** – Ask yourself: Why am I actually angry? Sometimes, anger is just frustration, hurt, or disappointment in disguise.
- **Express It Calmly** – Instead of yelling or lashing out, communicate your feelings in a clear, respectful way. Say "I feel upset because..." instead of attacking the other person.
- **Walk Away If Needed** – If your emotions are too intense, step away from the situation. Take a break, go for a walk, or listen to music to cool down.
- **Channel Anger into Something Positive** – Use exercise, writing, or a creative activity to release your emotions in a healthy way.

Handling Other Intense Emotions

1. When You Feel Sad or Disappointed

- Allow yourself to feel, but don't dwell on negativity.
- Talk to someone you trust instead of bottling it up.
- Focus on things you can control, rather than things you can't.

2. When You Feel Jealous or Insecure

- Instead of comparing yourself to others, focus on your growth.
- Use jealousy as motivation—what can you learn from others' success?
- Be grateful for what you do have instead of focusing on what you don't.

3. When You Feel Anxious or Stressed

- Breathe deeply—your body follows your breath.
- Break big tasks into small steps to avoid feeling overwhelmed.
- Remind yourself that most worries never actually happen.

You Are in Control: Your emotions are **not** your enemy. They are signals telling you something about your thoughts, your environment, and your life.

Instead of reacting impulsively, **learn to pause, reflect, and respond wisely.**

The difference between people who succeed and those who struggle isn't that they don't feel emotions—it's that they **control their emotions instead of letting their emotions control them.**

Next time you feel anger, sadness, or frustration, **take a deep breath and remind yourself: I have the power to choose how I react.**

Because **self-control is the real superpower.**

With belief in you,
AG

CHAPTER XI

The Importance of Mental Toughness

Dear Teenager,

Life is not always easy. There will be challenges, failures, and moments when you feel like giving up. But the one thing that will set you apart from others and help you succeed in life is **mental toughness.**

Mental toughness is the ability to stay strong, focused, and determined, even when things are difficult. It's what helps champions keep going after losing, entrepreneurs rise after failure, and students push through challenges to achieve their dreams.

Many people believe that success is about talent, luck, or intelligence. But in reality, the **people who succeed are those who refuse to quit, no matter how hard things get.**

Why Mental Toughness Matters

- **It helps you handle failure without giving up.**
- **It keeps you motivated when things get tough.**
- **It builds resilience, so you can bounce back stronger.**
- **It teaches you discipline, so you stay committed to your goals.**
- **It gives you emotional control, so you don't let stress or negativity stop you.**

How to Build Mental Toughness

1. **Develop a "Never Give Up" Attitude:** When things go wrong, don't quit—find another way. Every successful person has failed, but what made them different was that they kept going.

- Remind yourself: Quitting is not an option.
- When faced with failure, ask: What can I learn from this?
- Keep trying until you succeed.

2. **Train Your Mind to Stay Positive:** Your thoughts shape your reality. If you believe you can handle any challenge, you will. If you believe you are weak, you will struggle.

- Replace negative thoughts with positive ones.
- Say to yourself: "I can handle this. I will find a way."
- Avoid complaining and focus on solutions.

3. **Get Comfortable with Discomfort:** Success often requires stepping outside your comfort zone. The more you face difficult situations, the tougher you become.

- Challenge yourself to do something hard every day.
- Push through discomfort instead of running from it.
- When you feel like quitting, remind yourself: This is where growth happens.

4. Control Your Emotions: Mentally tough people don't let emotions control them. They feel emotions, but they respond wisely instead of reacting impulsively.

- Pause before reacting to difficult situations.
- Ask yourself: Is this worth my energy?
- Learn to stay calm under pressure.

5. Develop Self-Discipline: Mental toughness and discipline go hand in hand. If you can control your actions and build strong habits, success will follow.

- Stick to your goals, even when you don't feel like it.
- Wake up early, exercise, and work hard even when it's tough.
- Train yourself to stay focused, no matter the distractions.

6. See Challenges as Opportunities: Instead of seeing difficulties as obstacles, see them as chances to grow stronger.

- When you face a tough situation, ask: What can I learn from this?
- Remember: Every struggle makes you stronger.

Your Mind is Your Strongest Weapon

The most successful people are not the ones who had an easy life. They are the ones who faced difficulties, struggled, and kept going.

You have that same strength within you.

Next time you feel like giving up, remember: You are tougher than you think. You are capable of handling anything life throws at you.

Because true strength is not about muscles—it's about mental toughness.

With belief in you,
AG

CHAPTER XII

How to Overcome Fear & Self-Doubt

Dear Teenager,

Have you ever wanted to try something new but stopped yourself because of fear? Have you ever doubted your abilities, thinking "I'm not good enough," or "What if I fail?"

You are not alone. Fear and self-doubt affect everyone. Even the most successful people in the world have felt afraid at some point. The difference is, they didn't let fear stop them.

The good news is that fear and self-doubt are not permanent. You can train your mind to overcome them and build unstoppable confidence.

Why Do We Feel Fear & Self-Doubt?

1. **Fear of Failure** – Worrying about making mistakes or looking foolish.
2. **Fear of Judgment** – Thinking about what others will say or think.
3. **Fear of the Unknown** – Feeling uncomfortable about stepping into something new.
4. **Comparing Yourself to Others** – Thinking you're not as good as someone else.

These fears are normal, **but they only have power if you let them control you.**

How to Overcome Fear & Self-Doubt

1. Take Action, Even if You're Scared: Fear grows when you avoid things. The more you run from your fears, the stronger they become. The best way to beat fear? **Face it head-on.**

- Do the thing that scares you, even if it's uncomfortable.
- Start small—one step at a time.
- The more you face fear, the weaker it becomes.

Courage is not the absence of fear—it's taking action despite fear.

2. Reprogram Your Self-Talk: Your mind believes whatever you tell it. If you keep saying, "I can't do this," your brain will accept it as truth. Instead, start telling yourself:

- **"I am capable."**
- **"I will figure this out."**
- **"I have handled challenges before, and I can handle this too."**

What you say to yourself matters. **Speak to yourself like you would encourage a friend.**

3. Stop Worrying About What Others Think: Most people don't think about you as much as you imagine. They are too busy thinking about themselves!

- **Focus on your own growth instead of seeking approval.**
- **Realize that no one succeeds without making mistakes.**
- **Understand that people who judge you are not living your life—you are.**

4. See Failure as a Teacher, Not an Enemy: Fear of failure holds people back, **but failure is not the end—it's feedback.** Every successful person has failed multiple times.

- Instead of fearing failure, ask: "What can I learn from this?"
- Remember: Every mistake is a step forward if you learn from it.

5. Surround Yourself with Confident, Positive People: The people around you shape your mindset. If you're surrounded by negativity, fear, and self-doubt, you will absorb those emotions.

- Spend time with people who encourage you.
- Listen to podcasts, read books, and follow mentors who inspire confidence.
- Distance yourself from negative influences.

6. **Prepare, Then Trust Yourself:** Lack of confidence often comes from not being prepared. If you have an exam, speech, or challenge coming up, prepare well—then trust yourself.

- Train, practice, and improve your skills.
- But remember: **At some point, you have to stop overthinking and just go for it.**

7. **Visualize Success Instead of Failure:** Most people imagine the worst-case scenario. Flip that thinking. Visualize yourself succeeding.

Before a challenge, close your eyes and picture yourself doing well.
Feel the confidence as if you have already won.
This mental rehearsal tricks your brain into believing in your ability.

Fear is Temporary—Regret is Forever

Fear is a feeling—it will pass. But if you let fear stop you, you will regret the chances you didn't take.

So the next time fear or self-doubt tries to hold you back, **take a deep breath, remind yourself of your strength, and take action anyway.**

Because **the only way to truly fail is to never try.**

With belief in you,

AG

53

CHAPTER XIII

Dealing with Stress & Anxiety in a Fast-Paced World

Dear Teenager,

Life today moves faster than ever. You are constantly bombarded with **school pressures,social media, expectations from family, and the uncertainty of the future.** It's easy to feel overwhelmed, stressed, or anxious.

But here's the good news: **You have the power to manage stress and take control of your mind.** Stress is not the enemy—**not knowing how to handle it is.**

If you learn to manage stress early, you will become mentally stronger, more focused, and happier. Let's dive into how you can deal with stress and anxiety in a fast-paced world.

Why Do We Feel Stressed & Anxious?

Stress and anxiety happen when your mind feels overloaded. Some common reasons include:

- **School pressure** (exams, assignments, deadlines)
- **Comparison on social media** (feeling "not good enough")
- **Uncertainty about the future** (career, success, relationships)

- **Lack of time management** (feeling like there's too much to do)
- **Fear of failure or judgment**

While stress is normal, too much of it can lead to **burnout, anxiety, and even health problems.** That's why learning how to manage it is so important.

How to Deal with Stress & Anxiety

1. Take Control of Your Thoughts

Most stress comes from **how you think, not just what happens.**

- Instead of thinking "I have so much to do, I can't handle this," tell yourself: "I will do my best, one step at a time."
- Instead of "What if I fail?" say: "Even if I fail, I will learn and grow."
- Shift your mindset from **panic mode to problem-solving mode.**

2. Break Things Down—One Step at a Time

When you feel overwhelmed, it's usually because you're trying to do everything at once. **Slow down.**

- Write down what needs to be done.
- Prioritize the most important task.
- Focus on **one thing at a time** instead of worrying about everything.

3. Manage Your Time Wisely

Poor time management creates unnecessary stress.

- Plan your day—write a to-do list.
- Break big tasks into smaller, manageable steps.
- Avoid last-minute work—procrastination increases anxiety.

4. Disconnect from Social Media for Mental Peace

Social media can increase stress by making you compare your life with others.

- Limit social media time—take breaks from constant scrolling.
- Unfollow accounts that make you feel insecure or stressed.
- Remember: **People only show their highlights, not their struggles.**

5. Practice Deep Breathing & Relaxation Techniques

When stress hits, your body tenses up. **Breathing exercises can instantly calm your mind.**

- **The 4-7-8 method** – Inhale for 4 seconds, hold for 7 seconds, exhale for 8 seconds.
- **Progressive muscle relaxation** – Tighten and relax each part of your body, starting from your toes to your head.

- **Meditation & mindfulness** – Focus on the present moment instead of worrying about the future.

6. Move Your Body to Reduce Stress

Exercise is one of the best stress relievers.

- Go for a walk, jog, or play a sport.
- Stretch, do yoga, or hit the gym.
- Physical movement helps clear mental stress.

7. Get Enough Sleep

Lack of sleep increases anxiety and makes stress feel worse.

- Aim for 7-9 hours of sleep each night.
- Avoid screens 30 minutes before bed—blue light messes with sleep.
- Create a relaxing nighttime routine to calm your mind.

8. Talk to Someone You Trust

Bottling up stress makes it worse. Talking helps.

- Share your feelings with a trusted friend, family member, or mentor.
- Don't be afraid to ask for help—everyone needs support.
- If stress feels overwhelming, consider speaking to a counselor.

9. Focus on What You Can Control—Let Go of the Rest

A lot of stress comes from worrying about things you can't change.

- Ask yourself: "Is this within my control?"
- If yes—take action. If no—let it go and move forward.
- Train your mind to focus on solutions, not just problems.

10. Do Something That Brings You Joy

Stress can make you forget about the simple joys of life. Make time for things that make you happy.

- Listen to music, read, draw, or spend time in nature.
- Laugh—watch a funny video or talk to someone who makes you smile.
- Small moments of joy can refresh your mind and reduce stress.

Final Thought: You Are Stronger Than Your Stress

Stress and anxiety are part of life, but they don't have to control you. You are stronger than your worries. You have the power to manage your stress, calm your mind, and take control of your future.

So next time stress tries to take over, breathe, slow down, and remind yourself: "I can handle this."

With belief in you,
AG

59

CHAPTER XIV

The Power of Gratitude & Positive Thinking

Dear Teenager,

Life isn't always perfect. There will be struggles, disappointments, and challenges. But here's something powerful to remember: **your mindset determines how you experience life.**

Two people can go through the same situation—one feels defeated, while the other stays strong. **The difference?** Their perspective.

Gratitude and positive thinking are two of the most powerful tools you can develop. They can **change how you see the world, handle difficulties, and attract success into your life.**

Why Gratitude is Life-Changing

Gratitude means focusing on what you have rather than what you lack. It doesn't mean ignoring problems—it means choosing to see the good in every situation.

- **Gratitude shifts your focus from problems to possibilities.**
- **It makes you happier, reducing stress and anxiety.**

- **It helps you build better relationships by appreciating others.**
- **It boosts your motivation and self-confidence.**

How to Practice Gratitude Daily

1. **Start a Gratitude Journal** – Write 3 things you're grateful for each day.
2. **Say "Thank You" More Often** – Show appreciation to people who help you.
3. **Focus on What's Going Right** – Even on bad days, find small moments of joy.
4. **Appreciate Yourself** – Be grateful for your strengths, growth, and progress.

Gratitude isn't about having everything—it's about appreciating what you already have.

Why Positive Thinking is a Superpower

Your thoughts shape your reality. If you constantly think, "I'm not good enough" or "I will fail", your brain starts believing it. But if you replace those thoughts with "I am capable" or "I will find a way", your actions will reflect confidence and success.

What you focus on grows.

- If you focus on problems, they seem bigger.
- If you focus on solutions, you feel empowered.
- If you focus on failures, you lose motivation.

- If you focus on lessons, you grow stronger.

How to Develop a Positive Mindset

- **Catch Negative Thoughts** – When you think "I can't," pause and ask, "Why not?" Challenge your doubts.
- **Reframe Challenges** – Instead of "This is too hard," say "This is a chance to grow."
- **Surround Yourself with Positivity** – Be around people who uplift you, read inspiring books, and consume positive content.
- **Turn Setbacks into Comebacks** – Every failure teaches you something. Use it as fuel to move forward.

The Science of Gratitude & Positivity: Studies show that **grateful and positive people live happier, healthier, and more successful lives.** They have:

- Lower stress levels
- Better focus and problem-solving skills
- Stronger relationships
- More resilience in tough times

The best part? **Anyone can develop these habits.** It's not about ignoring reality but choosing to see **opportunities instead of obstacles.**

Your Mind is Your Power

You can choose to see the world through the lens of

problems or through the lens of gratitude and possibilities. **That choice shapes your life.**

Starting today, **train your mind to focus on the good, to appreciate what you have, and to believe in your ability to create a better future.**

Because when you develop gratitude and positive thinking, **nothing can break you.**

With belief in you,
AG

CHAPTER XV

How to Make Peace with Your Past & Move Forward

Dear Teenager,

Everyone has a past—mistakes made, people who hurt us, regrets that linger. Some of these experiences are painful, and it's easy to feel stuck in them. But here's something important to remember:

Your past does not define you. Your future is shaped by what you do today.

If you keep holding onto old pain, guilt, or regret, it will only weigh you down. To move forward and build a great life, you must learn to make peace with your past.

Why Do We Struggle to Let Go?

- We replay past mistakes, wishing we had done things differently.
- We hold onto anger toward people who hurt us.
- We feel ashamed or embarrassed about things we can't change.
- We compare ourselves to others and feel like we are behind.

But holding onto the past **does not change it.** It only stops you from enjoying the present and creating a better future.

How to Make Peace with Your Past

1. Accept That the Past Cannot Be Changed: No matter how much you think about it, the past will not rewrite itself. The only thing you control is how you **choose to move forward.**

- Stop wishing things were different.
- Accept that what happened, happened—but it doesn't have to define your future.
- Instead of saying "I wish I had done this differently," say "What can I learn from this?"

2. Forgive Yourself for Past Mistakes: Everyone makes mistakes. **Mistakes are how we grow.**

- Remind yourself that **you did the best you could with what you knew at the time.**
- Instead of feeling guilty, ask: "What did this teach me?"
- Use your past as **fuel to become better, not as a reason to feel stuck.**

3. Let Go of Resentment Toward Others: Holding onto anger or grudges **only hurts you, not them.**

- Forgiveness doesn't mean what they did was okay—it means **you refuse to let it control your happiness.**
- Don't let someone else's actions take away your peace.
- Free yourself from the burden of resentment and move forward.

4. Rewrite the Story You Tell Yourself: Instead of saying, "I have a bad past," reframe it as, "I have learned valuable lessons."

- Every experience, even painful ones, made you stronger and wiser.
- Focus on how far you've come, not just on what went wrong.
- **Your story is not over—the next chapter is in your hands.**

5. Focus on the Present & the Future: The best way to let go of the past is to create a future so exciting that you don't have time to dwell on old wounds.

- Set new goals for yourself—focus on **where you want to go, not where you've been.**
- Surround yourself with people who uplift and inspire you.
- Take daily actions that align with the person you want to become.

The Truth About Moving On

You don't move on in one day—it's a process. Some days will be harder than others, but each step forward counts.

And remember: You are not your past. You are who you choose to become.

So let go of the weight holding you back, forgive yourself, and move forward with strength and purpose. Your best days are ahead of you.

With belief in you,
AG

Part 3: Learning, Growth & Success

CHAPTER XVI

How to Build the Habit of Lifelong Learning

Dear Teenager,

Imagine if you had a superpower that allowed you to stay ahead in life, adapt to any challenge, and continuously grow. That superpower exists—it's called **lifelong learning.**

Most people stop learning once they finish school or college. They believe education is something that happens only in classrooms. But **the most successful and fulfilled people in the world never stop learning.**

Why Lifelong Learning is a Game-Changer

- It keeps your mind sharp and improves your thinking skills.
- It helps you adapt to new challenges and career changes.
- It makes you more confident and capable in life.
- It gives you a competitive advantage over those who stop learning.

The moment you stop learning, you stop growing. But if you make learning a habit, you will always be improving, evolving, and staying ahead.

How to Build the Habit of Lifelong Learning

1. **Read Every Day:** Reading is one of the best ways to learn. The most successful people in the world—Bill Gates, Elon Musk, Warren Buffett—are all avid readers.

- Read books on topics that interest you.
- Follow blogs, articles, and news that expand your knowledge.
- Listen to audiobooks or podcasts if you don't enjoy reading.

Even 10-15 minutes of reading a day can make a huge difference over time.

2. **Be Curious About Everything:** The world is full of things to learn—you just need curiosity.

- Ask questions: Why does this work like that? How can I do this better?
- Explore new topics: History, science, finance, self-improvement—anything that makes you smarter.
- Keep an open mind—learning happens when you're willing to see things from different perspectives.

3. **Learn from People, Not Just Books:** You can learn valuable lessons from people around you.

- Observe successful and inspiring people—what habits and skills do they have?
- Ask mentors, teachers, or family members for advice.

- Surround yourself with people who challenge you to grow.

4. Take Online Courses & Certifications: In today's digital world, you can learn anything online—often for free!

- Platforms like Coursera, Udemy, Khan Academy, and YouTube offer valuable knowledge.
- Learn new skills like coding, marketing, design, finance, or public speaking.
- Keep upgrading yourself—your future depends on the skills you build today.

5. Learn by Doing: The best way to learn is by taking action.

- If you want to learn about business, start a small project.
- If you want to improve public speaking, practice in front of a mirror or a small group.
- If you want to develop creativity, try writing, painting, or playing an instrument.

Experience is the best teacher. The more you do, the more you learn.

6. Teach What You Learn: One of the best ways to master a subject is to teach it to someone else.

- Share what you learn with friends or family.

- Start a blog, YouTube channel, or social media page to explain concepts to others.
- When you teach, you deepen your understanding.

7. **Stay Consistent – Learning is a Habit:** Just like exercising builds your body, learning builds your mind. Make it a daily habit.

Set aside 15-30 minutes every day for learning.
Track your progress—keep a notebook of what you've learned.
Enjoy the process—learning should feel exciting, not forced.

Your Future Depends on What You Learn Today

Lifelong learning is the key to **personal growth, career success, and a fulfilling life.** The world is changing fast—**those who keep learning will always stay ahead.**

So ask yourself: What's one new thing I can start learning today?

Because **the more you learn, the more you grow.**

With belief in you,
AG

CHAPTER XVII

Why School is Important (But Not Everything)

Dear Teenager,

You've probably heard people say, **"School is the key to success."** And while school is important, the truth is—**it's not everything.**

Yes, school teaches you valuable things like math, science, history, and language. It helps you develop discipline, teamwork, and responsibility. But **success in life is not just about getting good grades.**

Many of the world's most successful people—Elon Musk, Steve Jobs, Sachin Tendulkar, Ratan Tata—didn't succeed just because of school. **They succeeded because they kept learning beyond school.**

Why School is Important

1. **It Gives You Basic Knowledge:** You learn essential subjects that help you understand the world—math for managing money, science for logical thinking, history for understanding society.
2. **It Teaches Discipline & Hard Work:** Completing assignments, meeting deadlines, and studying for exams build work ethic—an important skill for success in life.

3. **It Helps You Build Social Skills:** You learn how to work with different people, handle group projects, and communicate effectively. These skills will help you in your career and relationships.
4. **It Opens Doors for Opportunities:** A good education can give you access to better universities, scholarships, and career options. It increases your chances of financial security.

But School is Not Everything

It May Not Teach You Life Skills: School teaches subjects, but it rarely teaches important skills like:

- **How to manage money (saving, investing, avoiding debt)**
- **How to handle failure & mental health**
- **How to develop confidence & communication skills**
- **How to think creatively & solve real-world problems**

These are things you need to learn **outside of school.**

Memorization is Not the Same as Intelligence: Many schools focus on **memorizing facts** instead of **understanding concepts.** But real intelligence is about applying knowledge, solving problems, and thinking critically—not just remembering answers for a test.

Your Grades Do Not Define You: Some of the most successful people in the world were not top students. **Success is about skills, hard work, and mindset—not just**

marks on a report card.

How to Make the Most of School (While Learning Beyond It)

1. Learn What Matters, Not Just What's Taught

- Pay attention to useful subjects (math, language, problem-solving).
- Don't just study for exams—understand how knowledge applies to real life.

2. Focus on Skills, Not Just Grades

- Develop skills like communication, leadership, and creativity.
- Learn how to think critically, not just follow instructions.

3. Start Learning Outside of School

- Read books on self-improvement, money, business, or psychology.
- Take online courses to build skills (coding, marketing, design, public speaking).
- Find mentors—talk to successful people and learn from them.

4. Take School Seriously, But Don't Let It Limit You

- Do your best in academics, but don't stress over every grade.
- Explore hobbies and interests outside of school.
- Real learning happens in experience, failure, and growth.

Education is Bigger Than School

School is a starting point, not the final destination. Real education happens when you take charge of your learning.

So, work hard in school—but don't stop there. Learn beyond textbooks, develop real skills, and create your own path to success.

Because school prepares you for exams, but life prepares you for success.

With belief in you,
AG

CHAPTER XVIII

The Truth About Passion & Career Choices

Dear Teenager,

You've probably heard the advice: **"Follow your passion, and you'll never work a day in your life."** It sounds inspiring, but is it really true?

The truth is, **passion alone is not enough** to build a successful and fulfilling career. Many people struggle because they believe they need to find their "one true passion" before they can succeed. But in reality, **passion is something you build, not just something you find.**

Let's break down the truth about passion and career choices.

Why Passion Alone is Not Enough

Passion Doesn't Always Pay the Bills: Loving something doesn't always mean it can be a career. You might love music, art, or gaming—but will people pay you for it? If not, you need to find a way to turn it into a valuable skill.

Passion Can Change Over Time: What you love today might not be what you love 10 years from now. Instead of looking for one lifelong passion, focus on building skills and exploring different interests.

Many Successful People Didn't Start with Passion: Most successful people didn't begin their careers by following their passion. Instead, they worked hard, got good at something, and passion followed success.

So, What Should You Focus on Instead?

1. Get Good at Something Valuable: Passion grows when you become **skilled at something and see its impact.**

- Identify careers that align with your interests AND have demand.
- Develop skills that people will pay for—public speaking, writing, coding, business, marketing, design, etc.
- Work hard to become great at your craft—when you're great at something, you start to love it.

2. Explore Different Paths: Most people don't "discover" their perfect career in one moment—they explore and figure it out along the way.

- Try internships, part-time jobs, or projects in different fields.
- Talk to people working in careers you admire.
- Keep learning—your dream career might be something you haven't even heard of yet!

3. Choose Growth & Purpose Over Just Passion: Instead of asking, **"What am I passionate about?"** ask:

- "What can I become really good at?"
- "What problems do I enjoy solving?"
- "What work will help me grow and make a difference?"

A career that challenges you and makes an impact will bring **far more satisfaction** than simply following a childhood passion.

4. Think About the Intersection of Passion, Skills & Demand: A great career happens when these three things align:

- **Passion** – Something you enjoy.
- **Skills** – Something you're good at or can become good at.
- **Demand** – Something the world needs and will pay for.

Find where these three meet, and you'll have a career that is **fulfilling AND financially stable.**

Passion is Built, Not Found

Your passion won't magically appear one day. It will develop as you explore, learn, and grow.

Instead of stressing over finding the "perfect career," focus on gaining skills, trying new things, and adding value to the world.

Because passion doesn't lead to success—success leads to

passion.

With belief in you,
AG

CHAPTER XIX

Why Your Skills Matter More Than Your Degree

Dear Teenager,

For years, people have been told that **getting a degree is the key to success.** But in today's world, that's only half the truth.

Yes, a degree can be valuable. It can open doors and help you get a job. But **your skills are what will determine how far you actually go in life.**

If you only have a degree but lack real-world skills, you might struggle. But if you have the right skills—even without a top degree—you can create incredible opportunities for yourself.

Why Skills Matter More Than Your Degree

1. The World is Changing Fast: Technology and industries are evolving quickly. Many jobs that exist today won't exist in 10 years. Employers no longer hire just based on degrees—they look for **people with real skills who can adapt and solve problems.**

A degree may get you in the door, but skills will keep you in the game.

2. Companies Hire for Skills, Not Just Degrees: Most companies care **more** about what you can do than where you studied. Employers want people who can:

- Communicate effectively
- Solve real-world problems
- Adapt to new challenges
- Think creatively and critically
- Work well in a team

A degree might list your education, but your skills prove your value.

3. Many Successful People Didn't Rely on Their Degrees

Look at some of the world's most successful people:

- Elon Musk (Tesla, SpaceX) – Self-taught engineering and business skills.
- Steve Jobs (Apple) – Dropped out of college but mastered design and innovation.
- Virat Kohli – No degree, but world-class cricket skills.
- Sachin Bansal & Binny Bansal (Flipkart founders) – Used skills in tech and business to build a billion-dollar company.

Their skills, not their degrees, built their success.

4. Skills Allow You to Create Your Own Opportunities: If you rely only on your degree, you're waiting for someone to **give you** an opportunity. But if you have skills, you can create your own path.

- Start freelancing (writing, design, marketing, coding).
- Launch your own business.
- Build projects, apps, or content that showcase your expertise.

The more skills you develop, the **more control you have over your future.**

5. Skills Make You Future-Proof: Industries change. Some degrees become outdated. But **skills never lose value.**

If you have strong skills, you will always be in demand.
You can switch careers if needed, because skills are transferable.
You stay ahead of those who only rely on a degree.

Essential Skills You Should Develop (No Matter Your Career Path)

Communication Skills – Learn to express ideas clearly and confidently.
Critical Thinking – Train yourself to solve problems logically.
Public Speaking – The ability to speak well opens doors everywhere.
Money Management – Learn how to budget, save, and invest early.
Digital Skills – Coding, design, content creation, or data analytics.
Sales & Persuasion – Being able to sell ideas or products is

a game-changer.

Networking & Relationship Building – Who you know can be just as important as what you know.

How to Develop Skills (Outside of College)

- Take Online Courses – Websites like Coursera, Udemy, and YouTube offer free and paid courses on high-demand skills.
- Internships & Freelancing – Gain real experience, not just classroom knowledge.
- Self-Learning – Read books, watch tutorials, and experiment on your own.
- Join Workshops & Networking Events – Learn from experts and connect with people.
- Start Small Projects – Build something—whether it's a blog, an app, a YouTube channel, or a small business.

Your Skills Will Define Your Success

Your degree may help, but **it is your skills that will set you apart.**

So don't just study for exams—**learn things that make you valuable.** Focus on developing skills that will help you grow, adapt, and thrive in the real world.

Because **in the end, what you can do matters more than what's written on a piece of paper.**

With belief in you,
AG

CHAPTER XX

The Power of Focus & Deep Work

Dear Teenager,

We live in a world full of distractions—smartphones buzzing, social media updates, endless notifications, and constant entertainment. **Staying focused has become harder than ever.**

But here's a secret: **The ability to focus deeply is one of the most powerful skills you can develop.**

If you can train your mind to concentrate without distractions, you will:

- Learn faster than others.
- Be more productive in less time.
- Get ahead in your studies and career.
- Feel a greater sense of achievement.

This is called **Deep Work**—the ability to focus without distractions on a task that challenges your brain. **It is a superpower in today's distracted world.**

Why Focus & Deep Work Matter

Focus Increases Productivity – You achieve more in less

time.

Deep Work Improves Creativity – Your best ideas come when you're fully engaged.

It Strengthens Your Brain – Just like muscles grow with exercise, focus strengthens your mind.

It Sets You Apart – In a world where most people are distracted, being focused gives you an advantage.

Why Most People Struggle to Focus

- Smartphones and Social Media – Constant notifications break concentration.
- Multitasking – Switching between tasks makes you less efficient.
- Lack of Training – Focus is a skill that must be developed, just like a muscle.
- Short Attention Span – Many people can't focus for more than a few minutes without getting distracted.

The good news? You can train yourself to focus deeply.

How to Master Focus & Deep Work

1. Train Your Brain to Work Without Distractions

- Set a timer for 30-60 minutes and work on one task without checking your phone.
- Start with small sessions and gradually increase your focus time.
- If you feel the urge to check your phone, resist it. You are training your brain to focus.

2. Use the Pomodoro Technique

- Work deeply for 25-45 minutes.
- Take a 5-10 minute break.
- Repeat the cycle 3-4 times, then take a longer break.
- This helps maintain high concentration levels without burning out.

3. Remove Distractions Before You Start

- Put your phone on Do Not Disturb mode.
- Work in a quiet space or use noise-canceling headphones.
- Block distracting websites if you're working on a computer.

4. Single-Task Instead of Multitasking

- Multitasking reduces focus and makes you less productive.
- Instead, focus on one task at a time—it will get done faster and better.

5. Plan Your Work & Prioritize Tasks

- Make a list of your most important tasks for the day.
- Tackle the hardest and most important work first (your brain is sharpest in the morning).

- Set clear goals before you start working—knowing what you need to do improves focus.

6. Train Your Mind Like a Muscle

- Start with short deep work sessions (30 minutes) and gradually increase them.
- The more you practice focus, the longer you will be able to concentrate.

7. Take Breaks to Recharge Your Mind

- After an hour of deep work, step away for 10-15 minutes.
- Go for a walk, stretch, or do a quick meditation to refresh your brain.
- Avoid using social media during breaks—it resets your distraction mode.

The Power of Deep Work in Real Life

People who master deep work achieve more in **weeks** than others do in **months**.

- Elon Musk builds rockets and electric cars because of his deep focus on engineering and problem-solving.
- Bill Gates used to take "Think Weeks," where he isolated himself to deeply focus on learning and strategy.
- Great athletes, artists, and leaders all practice deep work to master their skills.

Your Focus Determines Your Future

In a world full of distractions, **focus is the ultimate superpower.**

If you can train yourself to work deeply, you will get ahead of 90% of people who are constantly distracted.

So, starting today, **commit to building your focus muscle.** Train yourself to work deeply, and watch how your life transforms.

Because **success belongs to those who can focus in a world that can't.**

With belief in you,
AG

CHAPTER XXI

Time Management: The Superpower That Changes Lives

Dear Teenager,

Imagine if you had **24 extra hours every week** to do the things you love, learn new skills, and get ahead in life. Sounds amazing, right? The truth is, **you already have that time**—you just need to manage it better.

The most successful people in the world—whether athletes, entrepreneurs, or leaders—**don't have more time than you.** They just use their time **more wisely.**

If you master **time management**, you can:

- Get more done in less time.
- Reduce stress and last-minute rushing.
- Have time for things that truly matter.
- Achieve your goals faster than most people.

Why Most People Struggle with Time Management

Many teenagers (and adults) feel like they "never have enough time." But the real problem isn't **lack of time—it's poor time management.**

- Procrastination – Putting off important tasks until the last minute.
- Distractions – Social media, YouTube, and endless scrolling steal hours.
- No Clear Plan – Without a plan, time gets wasted on unimportant things.
- Multitasking – Trying to do too many things at once leads to poor results.

But the good news? **Time management is a skill, and you can master it!**

How to Manage Your Time Like a Pro

1. Plan Your Day Before It Starts

- Spend 5-10 minutes every morning (or the night before) planning your day.
- Write down the 3 most important tasks you need to complete.
- Break big tasks into smaller steps to avoid feeling overwhelmed.

Example: Instead of writing "Study for Math," write "Revise Chapter 5, Solve 10 Practice Questions."

2. Prioritize – Focus on What Matters Most

Not all tasks are equal. Some give huge results, while others are just busy work.

- Use the 80/20 Rule – 20% of your tasks create 80% of your success.
- Ask yourself: "Is this task really important, or am I just keeping busy?"
- Do high-impact tasks first—before wasting time on minor things.

3. Use the Pomodoro Technique for Focus

- Work deeply for 25-45 minutes (NO distractions).
- Take a 5-minute break after each session.
- Repeat this cycle 3-4 times, then take a longer break.

This keeps your brain fresh and helps you get more done in less time.

4. Avoid Time-Wasting Activities

Some things eat up time without adding value to your life.

- Endless scrolling on social media
- Binge-watching TV shows or YouTube videos
- Saying "yes" to everything and overloading yourself

Instead, replace these habits with productive ones—reading, learning a skill, or exercising.

5. Stop Multitasking – Focus on One Thing at a Time

Multitasking might seem productive, but it actually makes

you slower and less effective.

- Work on one task at a time with full focus.
- Finish it completely, then move on to the next.

You will get things done faster and with better quality.

6. Set Deadlines to Beat Procrastination

Procrastination happens when there's no urgency. Create deadlines for yourself!

- Give yourself fixed time limits for tasks.
- Use timers to create a sense of urgency.
- Reward yourself after completing important tasks.

Example: "I will finish my English essay by 4 PM, then reward myself with 30 minutes of my favorite show."

7. Use a Calendar or To-Do List

Keeping things in your head creates stress. Instead, write everything down.

- Use a planner, to-do list, or a simple notes app.
- Track deadlines for schoolwork, exams, and personal goals.
- Review your progress daily—adjust your plan if needed.

8. Say "No" to Things That Waste Your Time

You don't have to say yes to everything.

- If a task, event, or request doesn't add value to your life, learn to say NO.
- Protect your time like it's your most valuable resource—because it is!

Master Time, Master Life

The difference between people who succeed and those who struggle isn't **intelligence or luck—it's how they use their time.**

If you take control of your time, you take control of your life. **Start small, be consistent, and watch how your productivity, confidence, and success grow.**

Because **time is the most valuable thing you have—don't waste it.**

With belief in you,
AG

CHAPTER XXII

Money Lessons Every Teen Should Learn

Dear Teenager,

Most schools teach history, science, and math—but **they don't teach the most important subject: How to manage money.**

Many adults struggle with money because they never learned how to **save, invest, or manage their finances.** But if you start learning about money now, you'll be ahead of 90% of people.

Money isn't just about spending—it's about **freedom, security, and opportunities.** The earlier you learn smart money habits, the better your future will be.

Essential Money Lessons for Every Teen

1. Start Saving Money – Pay Yourself First: Saving is the foundation of financial success. No matter how much you earn, always save a portion of it.

- Follow the 50-30-20 Rule – Save at least 20% of any money you receive (allowance, gifts, part-time jobs).
- Treat saving like an expense – Set money aside before spending on other things.

- Small amounts add up – Saving ₹500 per month = ₹ 6,000 per year. Over time, this grows into a significant amount.

Golden Rule: It's not about how much you earn, but how much you keep.

2. Understand the Difference Between Needs & Wants: One of the biggest money mistakes people make is spending on things they don't really need.

Needs – Food, housing, education, basic clothes.
Wants – Latest gadgets, designer clothes, eating out frequently.

Before buying something, ask: "Do I really need this, or is it just a temporary desire?"
The more you save on unnecessary things now, the more financial freedom you'll have later.
Golden Rule: Live below your means, not just within them.

3. Learn to Budget – Control Where Your Money Goes: A budget is just a simple plan for how you use your money. Without one, it's easy to waste money and wonder where it all went.

- Track your income and expenses (use an app or a simple notebook).
- Set limits on spending for entertainment, shopping, and food.
- Stick to your budget and avoid impulse buying.

Golden Rule: If you don't control your money, your money will control you.

4. Stay Away from Debt – Credit Cards Are Not Free Money: Debt can ruin financial freedom. Many adults get trapped in credit card debt because they never learned how to use money wisely.

- If you don't have the money for something, don't buy it on credit.
- If you use a credit card, always pay the full amount before the due date to avoid high interest.
- Learn to be patient—save up for what you want instead of borrowing.

Golden Rule: Debt can make rich people richer and poor people poorer. Use it wisely.

5. Start Investing Early – Make Your Money Work for You: The biggest secret to building wealth is investing early. The earlier you start, the more your money grows over time.

- Learn about mutual funds, stocks, and index funds.
- Invest small amounts and watch them grow over time.
- Use the power of compound interest—where your money earns more money.

Example: If you invest ₹1,000 per month starting at 18, and it grows at 12% annually, you could have over ₹1 CRORE by the time you're 50!

Golden Rule: Invest early, invest smartly, and let your money grow.

6. Develop Multiple Sources of Income: Relying on just one income source (like a job) is risky. Smart people build multiple streams of income.

Freelancing – Learn skills like writing, graphic design, or coding.
Side Businesses – Sell something online, start a blog, or offer tutoring.
Investments – The best way to earn money without working is by letting investments grow.

Golden Rule: Never depend on just one income source—diversify your earnings.

7. Money Buys Freedom, Not Just Stuff: Many people waste money on expensive brands, gadgets, and luxury items to impress others. But the smartest people use money to buy freedom.

- Save and invest, so you don't have to work forever.
- Avoid lifestyle inflation—don't increase spending just because you earn more.
- Money gives you choices and independence—use it wisely.

Golden Rule: The goal is financial freedom, not just looking rich.

Be Smart with Money, and You'll Never Worry About It

The difference between people who struggle with money and those who build wealth is not their income—it's their habits.

Start practicing these money lessons today, and your future self will thank you.

Because if you learn how to manage money, you will never have to stress about it.

With belief in you,
AG

CHAPTER XXIII

Social Media: Your Best Friend or Your Worst Enemy?

Dear Teenager,

Social media is everywhere. It connects us, entertains us, and keeps us informed. But at the same time, it can **waste hours, damage confidence, and even control our emotions.**

The question is: **Is social media your best friend or your worst enemy?**

The answer depends on **how you use it.** Social media can be a powerful tool for learning, networking, and growing—or it can be a black hole of distraction, comparison, and negativity.

How Social Media Can Be Your Best Friend

It Connects You to the World

- You can talk to friends and family no matter where they are.
- You can meet like-minded people who share your interests.

It's a Powerful Learning Tool

102

- You can follow pages that teach you about career growth, business, science, or creativity.
- Platforms like YouTube and LinkedIn offer free education and skills development.

It Can Help You Build a Personal Brand

- You can showcase your talents (writing, photography, coding, public speaking, etc.).
- You can network with professionals who can guide you in your career.

It Can Inspire & Motivate You

- Following successful people can push you to set big goals.
- You can find mentors, business ideas, and personal development advice.

How Social Media Can Be Your Worst Enemy

It Wastes Your Time

- Hours of scrolling turn into an addiction without you realizing it.
- The more time spent online, the less time you have for real-life skills and growth.

It Creates Unrealistic Comparisons

- People only post their best moments, not their struggles.
- Comparing your life to others' highlights can make you feel like you're behind.

It Affects Mental Health

- Constant likes, comments, and validation create pressure.
- Cyberbullying, negativity, and fake news can increase anxiety and stress.

It Can Be a Distraction from Real Life

- Instead of focusing on real-world skills, friendships, and experiences, you might be stuck in a virtual world.
- Excessive screen time can affect sleep, focus, and relationships.

How to Use Social Media Wisely

1. Set Time Limits – Don't let social media control your day. Use it with purpose.
2. Follow the Right People – Unfollow toxic accounts and follow pages that inspire and educate.
3. Don't Compare Your Life to Others – Social media is a highlight reel, not real life.
4. Create More Than You Consume – Instead of just watching others, start creating—write, post, build a brand.

5. Take Social Media Detoxes – Spend time offline to stay connected with the real world.

The Social Media is a Tool—Use It, Don't Let It Use You

If used wisely, social media can help you grow, connect, and succeed. But if misused, it can waste time, harm self-esteem, and distract you from your real goals.

So, ask yourself: Is social media helping you or holding you back?

Because your future should be built by you, not by a screen.

With belief in you,
AG

Part 4: Relationships & Social Skills

CHAPTER XXIV

The Secret to Building Meaningful Friendships

Dear Teenager,

Friendships are one of the most valuable parts of life. The right friends bring **joy, support, and inspiration,** while the wrong ones can **drain your energy and hold you back.**

Many people have **hundreds of "friends" on social media but still feel lonely.** Why? Because real friendship isn't about numbers—it's about **quality.**

So, what's the secret to building **deep, meaningful friendships** that last?

1. Choose Your Friends Wisely: Your friendships will shape your habits, mindset, and future. **Surround yourself with people who lift you up, not pull you down.**

- Look for friends who support your growth, encourage your dreams, and bring positivity.
- Avoid people who constantly complain, gossip, or bring drama into your life.

Golden Rule: You become like the people you spend the most time with—so choose wisely.

2. Be a Great Friend First: If you want great friends, become the kind of person you'd want to be friends with.

- Listen more than you talk.
- Be honest, trustworthy, and supportive.
- Celebrate their successes instead of feeling jealous.

Golden Rule: Friendship is not about what you get—it's about what you give.

3. Prioritize Real Conversations Over Social Media: Many people chat online but never have deep conversations in real life. Real friendships grow through real connections.

- Call or meet up instead of just texting.
- Have meaningful conversations about life, goals, and struggles.
- Show up when your friend needs you, even if it's just to listen.

Golden Rule: Friendships grow when you invest time and effort in them.

4. Be Loyal & Trustworthy: The strongest friendships are built on trust and loyalty.

- Keep your promises.
- Don't gossip about your friends behind their backs.
- Stand by them in tough times, not just when things are fun.

Golden Rule: A real friend is someone who stays even when the rest of the world walks away.

5. Don't Be Afraid to Let Go of Toxic Friendships

Not all friendships are meant to last. If a friend constantly brings negativity, makes you feel bad about yourself, or takes more than they give, it's okay to walk away.

- Recognize the difference between a friend who helps you grow and one who holds you back.
- It's better to have a few true friends than a large circle of fake ones.

Golden Rule: Some friendships are lessons, some are lifelong—but all shape you in some way.

6. Learn to Forgive & Communicate: No friendship is perfect. There will be misunderstandings and disagreements. But strong friendships survive because of forgiveness and open communication.

- If there's a problem, talk about it instead of holding grudges.
- Say "sorry" when you're wrong, and be willing to forgive when your friend makes mistakes.
- True friendships are built on understanding, not perfection.

Golden Rule: Good friendships don't just happen—they are

built with patience and effort.

Friendships Shape Your Life

The right friends will bring out the best in you, inspire you, and make life more meaningful.

So, be intentional about who you surround yourself with, be the kind of friend you'd want in your life, and cherish the connections that truly matter.

Because life is too short for fake friendships—invest in the real ones.

With belief in you,
AG

CHAPTER XXV

How to Deal with Peer Pressure

Dear Teenager,

At some point in life, **everyone faces peer pressure**—the pressure to fit in, act a certain way, or do things just because "everyone else is doing it." It can come from friends, classmates, or even social media.

But here's the truth: **You don't have to follow the crowd to be accepted.** The strongest people in life are those who make their own choices, not those who blindly follow others.

Why Peer Pressure is Powerful

Peer pressure can be **positive or negative.**

Positive peer pressure – When friends encourage you to study, stay healthy, or take on new challenges.
Negative peer pressure – When people push you to do things that go against your values or better judgment.

The challenge is learning how to stand firm in your beliefs and make the right choices.

How to Handle Peer Pressure Like a Boss

1. Know Your Values & Stick to Them: If you don't know what you stand for, it's easy to be influenced by others.

- Ask yourself: What kind of person do I want to be?
- If something feels wrong, trust your instincts—you don't have to do it.
- Be proud of your beliefs, even if others think differently.

Golden Rule: When you stand for something, you won't fall for anything.

2. Learn to Say "No" With Confidence: Saying "no" doesn't make you weak—it makes you strong.

- Keep it simple: "No, I'm not interested."
- Change the subject or suggest something else: "Let's do something different instead."
- Walk away if needed—real friends won't force you to do things you're uncomfortable with.

Golden Rule: A true friend respects your choices, even if they are different from theirs.

3. Choose Friends Who Support You: Your closest friends should respect your decisions, not pressure you into bad ones.

- Surround yourself with people who encourage your growth.
- Distance yourself from toxic friends who pressure you into negative behavior.
- Remember: You become like the people you spend the most time with.

Golden Rule: Friends should lift you up, not push you down.

4. Think About the Consequences: Every choice you make has consequences.

Before making a decision, ask:

- Will I regret this later?
- Will this affect my future?
- Would I still do this if my parents or mentors were watching?

Peer pressure fades, but bad choices can have long-term effects.

Golden Rule: Think long-term—don't let a moment of pressure ruin your future.

5. Be a Leader, Not a Follower: People admire those who have the courage to make their own decisions.

- Set an example by making smart choices.
- Be the friend who encourages others to do what's right.
- Lead with confidence—others might follow your strength.

Golden Rule: The world needs more leaders, not more followers.

6. Have an Exit Strategy: If you ever feel pressured, have a plan to remove yourself from the situation.

- Use an excuse: "I have to go, my parents need me."
- Call a trusted friend or family member for support.
- If you're uncomfortable, leave immediately.

Golden Rule: You don't owe anyone an explanation for protecting your values.

Your Choices Define You

You have the power to choose your own path. Never let peer pressure push you into being someone you're not.

The people who truly matter will respect you for being yourself.

So next time you face peer pressure, stand tall, stay strong, and make the choice that's right for you.

Because your future is too important to let someone else control it.

With belief in you,
AG

CHAPTER XXVI

The Importance of Family in Your Life

Dear Teenager,

In a world where friendships, trends, and social media are constantly changing, there is one thing that remains **constant—your family.**

Family is not just about blood relations; it's about **the people who love, support, and guide you through life.** They are the ones who truly care about you, even when the rest of the world doesn't.

As you grow, you may sometimes feel like your family **doesn't understand** you or that friends are more important. But as life goes on, you'll realize that **family is the foundation that shapes you.**

Why Family is So Important

1. They Love You Unconditionally: Your family loves you not because of what you do, but because of who you are.

- Friends may come and go, but family stands by you.
- No matter how many mistakes you make, your family will always want the best for you.
- Even when they correct you, it's because they care.

Golden Rule: You may not always agree with your family,

but they are the ones who will always have your back.

2. They Teach You Life's Most Important Lessons: Most of what you learn about morals, values, and relationships comes from your family.

- They teach you respect, honesty, and responsibility.
- They show you how to handle problems, failures, and challenges.
- They help you become a better version of yourself.

Golden Rule: Family prepares you for the real world in ways you don't even realize.

3. They Are Your Strongest Support System: When life gets tough, your family is your safe space.

- When you're feeling lost, they help you find direction.
- When you fail, they encourage you to try again.
- When you succeed, they celebrate with you.

Golden Rule: True success feels empty if you have no one to share it with—family makes every moment meaningful.

4. They Shape Your Identity & Culture: Your family gives you a sense of belonging.

- They pass down traditions, values, and history.
- They help you understand who you are and where you come from.

- They give you a foundation to stand on as you create your own path.

Golden Rule: Understanding your roots helps you grow stronger.

5. They Are the Ones Who Truly Want You to Succeed: Many people will come into your life for their own benefit, but your family genuinely wants to see you win.

- Parents sacrifice so much just to give you opportunities.
- Siblings may annoy you, but they will always stand by you.
- Grandparents, uncles, and aunts pass down wisdom that can guide you for life.

Golden Rule: The people who invest in your growth deserve your love and respect.

How to Strengthen Your Relationship with Your Family

1. Spend time with them – Don't always stay locked in your room or on your phone.
2. Talk to them – Share your dreams, struggles, and experiences.
3. Respect them – Even if you don't always agree, show appreciation for their efforts.
4. Forgive and move on – No family is perfect, but holding grudges only hurts you.
5. Be there for them – Just like they are always there for you.

Family is Your Greatest Treasure

As you grow older, you'll realize that fame, money, and success come and go—but family is forever.

Cherish them, love them, and never take them for granted. When everything else fades, family remains.

With love and belief in you,
AG

CHAPTER XXVII

Why Respecting Others Opens Doors for You

Dear Teenager,

Respect is one of the most powerful traits you can develop. It costs nothing, yet it can open doors, build strong relationships, and create opportunities that you never imagined.

In a world where people are often self-centered, **those who show genuine respect stand out.** Whether it's in school, at home, in friendships, or in your future career, **respecting others will take you further than talent alone.**

What Does Respect Really Mean?

Respect isn't just about being polite—it's **about how you treat people, regardless of who they are.**

- Listening to others without interrupting.
- Valuing different opinions, even when you disagree.
- Being kind and courteous to everyone, not just those in power.
- Treating people with dignity, whether they are rich, poor, young, or old.

Golden Rule: Treat others the way you want to be treated.

How Respect Opens Doors for You

1. People Will Want to Help You: When you treat people with respect, they remember you. **Teachers, mentors, and professionals** are more likely to guide and support those who are polite and appreciative.

- A kind word to a teacher can get you extra guidance.
- Respecting classmates can build lifelong friendships.
- Being polite to strangers can lead to unexpected opportunities.

Golden Rule: The way you treat people today can determine who will help you tomorrow.

2. Respect Earns You Trust & Influence: The most respected people in the world are not those who demand authority, but those who earn it through humility and kindness.

- When you show respect, people trust you more.
- Leaders who respect others gain influence effortlessly.
- Respect creates stronger, healthier relationships in life and work.

Golden Rule: If you want to be respected, start by respecting others.

3. It Helps You Avoid Unnecessary Conflict: Disrespect creates drama, tension, and broken relationships. Respect prevents misunderstandings and keeps things peaceful.

- Even if someone is rude, stay calm and respond with respect.
- If you disagree with someone, do it respectfully—not by insulting them.
- Respectful people rarely get into unnecessary fights or trouble.

Golden Rule: The strongest person in the room is the one who stays respectful even when others don't.

4. It Makes You More Likable & Approachable: Nobody enjoys being around someone who is arrogant, rude, or dismissive. However, respectful people naturally attract friends, mentors, and opportunities.

- Being kind and respectful makes you someone people enjoy talking to.
- It helps you build a strong network of friends and supporters.
- People remember and recommend those who treat others well.

Golden Rule: Your reputation is built by how you treat people.

5. It Prepares You for Success in Work & Life: In your future career, respect will be just as important as your skills. Employers hire, promote, and recommend people who treat others well.

- The way you treat waiters, cleaners, or strangers reveals your true character.
- The best bosses and leaders are those who respect their teams.
- Respect leads to better teamwork, stronger leadership, and more career growth.

Golden Rule: People may forget what you said, but they will never forget how you made them feel.

How to Show Respect in Everyday Life

1. Listen before speaking – Give people your full attention.
2. Say "thank you" and "please" – Small words make a big difference.
3. Respect different opinions – You don't have to agree with everyone, but you can still be kind.
4. Treat everyone with dignity – Whether it's a friend, teacher, stranger, or worker.
5. Avoid gossip and insults – Negative talk harms both you and others.

Respect Opens More Doors Than You Can Imagine

The world rewards those who treat others well. Respect will bring you opportunities, friendships, and success in ways you never expected.

So, starting today, choose to be someone who lifts others up, not tears them down. Because respect isn't just about how you treat others—it's about who you become.

With belief in you,
AG

CHAPTER XXVIII

How to Communicate with Confidence & Clarity

Dear Teenager,

Communication is one of the most powerful skills you can develop. Whether you're speaking in class, expressing your ideas, or having everyday conversations, **how you communicate affects how people see you.**

The good news? **Confidence in communication is a skill you can develop.** Even if you feel shy or nervous, you can learn to speak with clarity, power, and impact.

Here's how.

Why Confident Communication Matters

- It helps you express your ideas clearly.
- It makes people take you seriously.
- It boosts your confidence in school, work, and social life.
- It helps you make strong first impressions.

Golden Rule: If you can communicate well, you can influence, inspire, and succeed.

How to Communicate with Confidence & Clarity

1. Believe in What You're Saying: Confidence starts in your mind. If you don't believe in your own words, neither will others.

- Know your topic – If you're speaking about something, understand it well.
- Trust your voice – Your opinion matters. Speak with conviction.
- Stop doubting yourself – You don't need to be perfect to speak confidently.

Golden Rule: Confidence in speaking comes from confidence in yourself.

2. Speak Slowly & Clearly: When you rush your words, you seem nervous. Slow down, pause, and speak with clarity.

- Take deep breaths before speaking.
- Avoid filler words like "um," "uh," and "like" too often.
- Pronounce words clearly—don't mumble.

Golden Rule: The more clearly you speak, the more confidently you'll be heard.

3. Use Strong Body Language: Your words matter, but how you say them matters even more.

- Stand or sit up straight—don't slouch.
- Make eye contact instead of looking down.
- Use hand gestures naturally, but don't overdo them.

Golden Rule: Your body language should show confidence, not insecurity.

4. Listen Before You Speak: Great communicators are also great listeners. Pay attention to others before responding.

- Show interest by nodding and maintaining eye contact.
- Don't interrupt—let people finish their thoughts.
- Take a moment to think before you reply.

Golden Rule: Listening makes your words more powerful.

5. Improve Your Vocabulary & Expression: The more words you know, the easier it is to express yourself.

- Read books, listen to speeches, and expand your knowledge.
- Learn new ways to say things instead of repeating the same phrases.
- Practice explaining your thoughts clearly.

Golden Rule: Strong vocabulary = Stronger communication.

6. Practice, Practice, Practice: Like any other skill, confident communication gets better with practice.

- Speak in front of a mirror to improve body language.
- Record yourself and listen to how you sound.
- Engage in discussions with friends or family.

Golden Rule: The more you speak, the more natural it becomes.

7. Handle Nervousness Like a Pro: Feeling nervous is normal. But you can train yourself to stay calm.

- Take deep breaths before speaking.
- Focus on the message, not on yourself.
- Remind yourself: "I have something valuable to say."

Golden Rule: Confidence is not about never feeling nervous—it's about speaking despite it.

Your Voice is Powerful—Use It Well

The way you communicate shapes your future. If you can speak with confidence and clarity, you can inspire, influence, and make an impact.

So, start today. Believe in your words, practice speaking, and never be afraid to express yourself.

Because your voice deserves to be heard.

With belief in you,
AG

CHAPTER XXIX

Handling Conflicts Like a Wise Person

Dear Teenager,

Conflict is a part of life. Whether it's with friends, family, teachers, or even strangers, disagreements happen. But **how you handle conflict defines your character.**

Some people react with **anger** and make things worse. Others avoid conflict and never solve their problems. But **wise people handle conflicts calmly, with understanding and respect.**

Here's how you can deal with conflicts like a wise person.

1. Stay Calm – Don't React Emotionally: When conflict arises, your first instinct may be to get angry or defensive. But reacting with emotion often makes things worse.

- Take a deep breath before responding.
- Pause and ask yourself: "Is this worth fighting over?"
- Respond with a clear mind, not just emotions.

Golden Rule: The calmer you are, the more control you have over the situation.

2. Listen Before Speaking: Many conflicts escalate because people don't listen to each other.

Let the other person speak first—really try to understand their point.

Don't interrupt or assume you already know what they're saying.

Repeat their point in your own words to show you're listening.

Golden Rule: People want to be heard—respect them by listening first.

3. Choose Your Words Wisely: What you say in a conflict can either solve the issue or make it worse.

- Don't use insults, sarcasm, or harsh words.
- Speak respectfully, even if you're upset.

Instead of blaming, use "I" statements:

- "You never listen to me!"
- "I feel unheard when we argue."

Golden Rule: Speak to solve, not to hurt.

4. Try to Understand the Other Person's Perspective

Often, conflicts arise from misunderstandings.

- Ask yourself: "Why is this person upset? What's really bothering them?"
- Put yourself in their shoes—how would you feel if you were them?

- Show empathy by saying: "I understand where you're coming from."

Golden Rule: When you understand people, you can resolve conflicts faster.

5. Know When to Walk Away: Not every conflict is worth fighting over.

- If someone is being unreasonable, don't waste energy arguing.
- If tempers are too high, suggest discussing it later.
- Some battles are best left alone—focus on what truly matters.

Golden Rule: Sometimes, walking away is the smartest move.

6. Find a Solution, Not Just a Winner: The goal of handling conflict is not to "win" the argument but to find a fair solution.

- Instead of proving you're right, ask: "How can we fix this?"
- Look for compromises where both sides benefit.
- Remember: Relationships matter more than being "right."

Golden Rule: A wise person focuses on solutions, not ego.

7. Apologize When You're Wrong: Many conflicts continue because people refuse to admit their mistakes.

- If you made a mistake, own up to it.
- A simple "I'm sorry" can end a fight faster than anything else.
- Apologizing doesn't make you weak—it shows maturity and strength.

Golden Rule: A sincere apology can heal even the biggest conflicts.

Conflict is a Test of Your Wisdom

How you handle conflict shows your true character. Will you react with anger, or will you respond with wisdom?

Choose to stay calm, listen, and find solutions. Because wise people don't fight to win—they resolve to grow.

With belief in you,
AG

CHAPTER XXX

Why Trust is the Most Valuable Currency in Life

Dear Teenager,

In a world where money, fame, and success often seem like the most important things, there's something far more valuable: **Trust.**

Trust is the foundation of every relationship—whether it's with family, friends, teachers, or even your future career. **Once you lose trust, it's very hard to get it back.** But if people trust you, **opportunities, friendships, and success will follow naturally.**

Why Trust is More Valuable Than Money

- **Money can be lost and earned back.**
- **Words are easy to say.**
- **But trust, once broken, is hard to rebuild.**

- **Trust makes people believe in you.**
- **Trust opens doors that money can't.**
- **Trust helps you build strong relationships that last a lifetime.**

Golden Rule: Without trust, nothing meaningful in life can be built.

How to Earn Trust & Keep It

1. Keep Your Promises: People trust those who **do what they say they will do.**

- If you say you'll do something, follow through.
- If you can't keep a promise, be honest and communicate.
- Avoid making promises just to please others.

Golden Rule: Your word is your reputation—honor it.

2. Be Honest, Even When It's Hard: Lies can destroy trust instantly. Even small lies create doubt in people's minds.

- Always tell the truth, even if it's uncomfortable.
- If you make a mistake, admit it instead of covering it up.
- People respect honesty—even when the truth isn't perfect.

Golden Rule: Honesty may be difficult in the moment, but it builds lifelong trust.

3. Be Reliable & Dependable: People trust those they can count on.

- Show up on time and be consistent.
- Finish what you start and take responsibility for your actions.

- Avoid being flaky or unreliable—your reliability defines your character.

Golden Rule: If people know they can count on you, they will trust you more.

4. Keep Confidences – Be Trustworthy with Secrets: If someone trusts you with personal information, respect that trust.

- Never gossip or share someone's secrets.
- Be the kind of person people feel safe talking to.
- If you accidentally hurt someone's trust, apologize sincerely.

Golden Rule: Trust is built in years but lost in seconds—protect it.

5. Admit When You're Wrong & Make Things Right: Nobody is perfect. But the way you handle mistakes determines your trustworthiness.

- If you mess up, own it instead of making excuses.
- Apologize sincerely and take action to fix things.
- Avoid blaming others—take responsibility.

Golden Rule: People don't expect perfection, but they do expect honesty and accountability.

How Trust Opens Doors for You

- In Friendships – Trust makes your relationships deeper and more meaningful.
- In Your Career – Employers hire and promote those they can trust.
- In Business – Customers and clients stick with companies they trust.
- In Life – Trust makes people believe in you, support you, and want to help you succeed.

Protect Your Trust Like Gold

Once you earn trust, guard it carefully.
Once you break trust, it's hard to regain.

So be honest, reliable, and true to your word—because trust is the real currency of life.

With belief in you,
AG

Part 5: Purpose, Passion & Happiness

CHAPTER XXXI

Finding Your Purpose in Life

Dear Teenager,

At some point, you might ask yourself: **"What am I meant to do in life?"** or **"How do I find my purpose?"**

The truth is, **finding your purpose isn't about waking up one day with all the answers.** It's a journey—one that requires exploration, self-discovery, and growth.

But here's what you need to know: **You already have a purpose. You just need to uncover it.**

Why Finding Your Purpose Matters

- Gives Meaning to Life – Purpose helps you feel fulfilled and driven.
- Helps You Make Better Choices – When you know what you stand for, decisions become easier.
- Keeps You Motivated – Even when challenges arise, a strong purpose helps you push through.
- Allows You to Make an Impact – Purpose isn't just about you—it's about how you can contribute to the world.

Golden Rule: A life without purpose is like a ship without direction—it drifts aimlessly.

How to Find Your Purpose

1. Pay Attention to What Excites You: Your purpose often hides in the things that light you up.

- What topics make you curious?
- What activities make you lose track of time?
- What do you naturally enjoy doing?

Golden Rule: What excites you is a clue to what you're meant to do.

2. Explore Different Interests & Skills: You won't find your purpose by just thinking—you have to explore.

- Try new hobbies, subjects, and experiences.
- Develop skills that challenge and excite you.
- Don't be afraid to fail—every experience teaches you something.

Golden Rule: You don't "find" purpose by waiting—you discover it by doing.

3. Ask Yourself: What Problems Do I Want to Solve?

Purpose isn't just about what you love—it's about how you can make a difference.

- What problems in the world do you care about?
- How can your skills help others?
- What impact do you want to leave behind?

Golden Rule: True purpose is found in serving something bigger than yourself.

4. Learn from People Who Inspire You: Look at those who have found their purpose—what can you learn from them?

- Read books or watch interviews of successful, purpose-driven people.
- Find mentors who can guide you.
- Surround yourself with people who challenge and inspire you.

Golden Rule: Success leaves clues—learn from those who've walked the path before you.

5. Don't Stress About Having It All Figured Out

Your purpose may change over time—and that's okay.

- You don't need to have all the answers today.
- Focus on growing, learning, and evolving.
- Trust that, over time, your purpose will become clearer.

Golden Rule: Your purpose is not a destination—it's a lifelong journey.

Live with Purpose Every Day

Instead of waiting for some "big revelation," start living with purpose today.

Do things that matter.
Keep learning and growing.
Make an impact in small ways—kindness, effort, and passion all count.

Because when you focus on living with purpose every day, your bigger purpose will naturally unfold.

With belief in you,
AG

CHAPTER XXXII

The True Meaning of Happiness

Dear Teenager,

What does it really mean to be happy? Is it about having lots of money? Owning the latest gadgets? Getting thousands of likes on social media?

The world often tells us that happiness comes from **external things—success, fame, wealth,** or approval from others. But the truth is, **real happiness comes from within.**

What Happiness is NOT

- It's NOT about having everything you want. Many rich, famous people are still unhappy.
- It's NOT about avoiding problems. Life will always have challenges.
- It's NOT about what others think. Happiness is personal—it's about how you feel inside.

Golden Rule: If your happiness depends on things outside of you, you will always feel like something is missing.

What True Happiness Really Is

1. Happiness is Finding Joy in the Present: Many people say, "I'll be happy when I get a better job, more money, or more success." But happiness isn't something you find in the future—it's something you create right now.

- Appreciate the little things—laughter with friends, a good book, a peaceful moment.
- Stop waiting for "one day" to be happy—enjoy life as it is.
- Gratitude turns what you have into enough.

Golden Rule: If you can't be happy with what you have now, you won't be happy with more.

2. Happiness Comes from Meaning, Not Just Pleasure: Pleasure is temporary—it fades. True happiness comes from living a meaningful life.

- Do things that matter—help others, grow, and contribute.
- Work toward a purpose bigger than yourself.
- Focus on who you are becoming, not just what you are getting.

Golden Rule: Chasing pleasure brings momentary highs—finding purpose brings lasting joy.

3. Happiness is Inner Peace, Not Just Excitement: Being happy doesn't mean being excited all the time. Sometimes, happiness is calmness, contentment, and knowing you are on the right path.

- Let go of negativity—don't let small things steal your peace.

- Accept that some days will be tough—but that doesn't mean life is bad.
- Stop overthinking—sometimes, happiness is just being present.

Golden Rule: Happiness is not the absence of problems, but the ability to deal with them peacefully.

4. Happiness is Being True to Yourself: Many people feel unhappy because they are trying to please others instead of being themselves.

- Don't live for other people's approval.
- Do what makes YOU feel fulfilled—not just what is popular.
- Choose relationships, careers, and goals that align with your values.

Golden Rule: You can't be truly happy if you're pretending to be someone you're not.

How to Cultivate Happiness Every Day

- Practice gratitude – Write down 3 things you're thankful for every day.
- Take care of yourself – Sleep, exercise, eat well, and prioritize mental health.
- Give more than you take – Helping others brings deep, lasting joy.
- Focus on experiences, not things – The best memories come from moments, not money.

- Surround yourself with positive people – Energy is contagious—choose wisely.

Happiness is a Choice

Happiness isn't something you find—it's something you create.

The secret? Live with gratitude, meaning, and authenticity. Stop chasing happiness and start practicing it every day.

Because the happiest people aren't those who have the most—they are those who appreciate the most.

With belief in you,
AG

CHAPTER XXXIII

The Importance of Giving & Helping Others

Dear Teenager,

In a world that often tells you to focus on **what you can get**, there's a deeper truth: **True happiness and success come from what you give.**

Helping others isn't just about kindness—it **changes your life, your mindset, and your future.**

Why Giving Matters

- It Makes You Happier – Studies show that people who help others feel more fulfilled and joyful.
- It Builds Stronger Relationships – People trust, respect, and appreciate those who give without expecting anything in return.
- It Creates a Positive Impact – Even small acts of kindness can change someone's life.
- It Makes You a Better Leader – The greatest leaders are those who serve others first.
- It Brings Purpose to Life – Life feels more meaningful when you contribute to something bigger than yourself.

Golden Rule: The more you give, the richer your life becomes—not just in money, but in love, purpose, and fulfillment.

Ways to Give & Help Others

1. Give Your Time: You don't need money to give—your time is just as valuable.

- Volunteer at a local school, charity, or community event.
- Help a friend, sibling, or classmate with something they're struggling with.
- Spend time with people who need support—sometimes, listening is the greatest gift.

Golden Rule: Your time and presence are gifts that money can't buy.

2. Share Your Knowledge & Skills: What you know can help others grow.

- Teach a younger sibling or friend something new.
- If you're good at a subject, help classmates who are struggling.
- Share your talents—whether it's music, art, writing, or sports—to inspire others.

Golden Rule: Knowledge grows when it's shared.

3. Offer Kindness & Encouragement: Words have power—use them to lift others up.

Give someone a genuine compliment.

Encourage someone who's going through a tough time. Smile, be kind, and treat people with respect—even when no one's watching.

Golden Rule: Kindness costs nothing but means everything.

4. Give Without Expecting Anything in Return: True generosity is giving without looking for rewards.

- Help not because you have to, but because you want to.
- Don't expect praise or something in return—give because it feels right.
- Remember: Even small acts of giving create ripples that can change the world.

Golden Rule: Give with a full heart, and the world will give back in ways you never expect.

The Secret: Giving Helps YOU Too

Many people think giving is about helping others, but the truth is—it transforms YOU the most.

- You feel happier and more fulfilled.
- You gain respect and trust from others.
- You become a person of value in your community.
- You develop leadership, empathy, and a mindset of abundance.

Life is About What You Give, Not Just What You Get

The people who are truly happy and successful in life aren't the ones who take the most. They are the ones who give the most.

So, ask yourself every day: "How can I help someone today?"

Because when you lift others up, you rise too.

With belief in you,
AG

CHAPTER XXXIV

Why Self-Discipline Leads to Freedom

Dear Teenager,

You might think **freedom** means doing whatever you want, whenever you want. But the truth is, **real freedom comes from self-discipline.**

At first, discipline sounds like **rules and restrictions**—but in reality, it's the key to achieving your dreams, controlling your life, and becoming truly free.

What is Self-Discipline?

Self-discipline is **your ability to control your actions, emotions, and habits** to achieve a bigger goal.

- It's choosing:
- Long-term success over short-term pleasure.
- Hard work over laziness.
- Doing what's right, even when you don't feel like it.

Golden Rule: Discipline is doing what needs to be done, even when you don't want to do it.

How Self-Discipline Leads to Freedom

1. It Gives You Control Over Your Life: Without discipline, life controls you—your moods, distractions, and bad habits decide what you do. With discipline, YOU are in control.

- You wake up early instead of hitting snooze.
- You focus on your goals instead of wasting time.
- You build healthy habits instead of being ruled by impulses.

Golden Rule: The more you control yourself, the less others control you.

2. It Helps You Achieve Your Dreams: Many people want success, but few have the discipline to work for it.

Athletes train daily, even when they don't feel like it.
Entrepreneurs work hard before they see results.
Students who stay focused get ahead in life.

Golden Rule: Your dreams don't work unless you do.

3. It Frees You from Regret & Stress: Lack of discipline leads to:

- Missed opportunities.
- Last-minute panic before deadlines.
- Regret over wasted time.

When you're disciplined, you feel in control, stress-free, and confident about your future.

Golden Rule: Discipline now = peace later.

4. It Builds Financial & Personal Freedom

- Want financial freedom? You need discipline in spending and saving.
- Want a great body? You need discipline in exercise and eating.
- Want a strong mind? You need discipline in learning and growth.

Self-discipline is the bridge between where you are and where you want to be.

Golden Rule: The disciplined few achieve what the undisciplined many only dream of.

How to Develop Self-Discipline

Start Small – Set small, achievable goals every day.

- Remove Temptations – Limit distractions (social media, junk food, negativity).
- Follow a Routine – A daily schedule keeps you consistent.
- Do the Hard Things First – Train your mind to tackle challenges.
- Stay Consistent – Discipline is built through repetition.

Discipline = Freedom

At first, self-discipline feels like a restriction—but in time, it becomes your greatest power.

It gives you control, success, confidence, and

freedom—while others stay stuck in bad habits.

So, choose discipline today, and enjoy true freedom tomorrow.

With belief in you,
AG

CHAPTER XXXV

The Balance Between Dreams & Reality

Dear Teenager,

You've been told to **dream big, chase your passion, and believe in yourself.** And that's important—**dreams give life meaning.** But here's something most people don't tell you:

Dreaming isn't enough. You also need to **stay grounded in reality.**

The secret to success isn't just having big dreams—it's balancing them with **action, hard work, and practical thinking.**

Why Both Dreams & Reality Matter

- **Dreams give you vision and motivation.**
- **Reality teaches you discipline and strategy.**
- **Balancing both helps you turn dreams into achievements.**

Golden Rule: A dream without action is just a wish. Reality without dreams is just survival.

How to Balance Dreams & Reality

1. Dream Big, But Start Small: Many people dream of success but never take the first step.

- Set ambitious goals, but break them down into smaller, achievable steps.
- Focus on daily progress, not instant results.
- Ask yourself: What can I do today that brings me closer to my dream?

Golden Rule: Success is built one step at a time.

2. Be Realistic About Challenges

Dreaming is easy—facing challenges is the hard part.

- Understand that failure, rejection, and obstacles are part of the journey.
- Don't quit when things get tough—adjust and keep going.
- Learn from setbacks instead of seeing them as reasons to give up.

Golden Rule: The dreamers who succeed are the ones who refuse to quit.

3. Take Action Every Day

You can't just dream—you have to put in the work.

- Want to be a writer? Write something every day.
- Want to be an athlete? Train consistently.

- Want to start a business? Learn about it, take small risks, and build experience.

Golden Rule: Dreams come true when action meets consistency.

4. Stay Adaptable – Life Doesn't Always Go as Planned

Sometimes, things won't go exactly how you imagined. That's okay.

- Be flexible—if one path doesn't work, find another way.
- Learn new skills and be open to different opportunities.
- Growth happens when you step out of your comfort zone.

Golden Rule: Success isn't about sticking to one plan—it's about adapting when needed.

5. Surround Yourself with the Right People

The people around you will influence your dreams and your reality.

- Stay close to those who encourage and challenge you.
- Avoid people who constantly bring negativity and doubt.
- Seek mentors who have already achieved what you aspire to.

Golden Rule: Your environment shapes your future—choose it wisely.

Dream, Plan, and Execute

Dreams give you direction. Reality gives you the tools to get there.

So dream fearlessly, work relentlessly, and stay grounded in reality. Because when dreams and reality meet, success is born.

With belief in you,
AG

CHAPTER XXXVI

Chasing Success vs. Chasing Meaning

Dear Teenager,

Most people grow up believing that **success is the ultimate goal.** Society tells us that success means **money, fame, power, or status.** But have you ever wondered—**what if success alone isn't enough?**

There's a deeper question to ask: **Do you want to chase success, or do you want to chase meaning?**

The Difference Between Success & Meaning

Chasing Success

- Focuses on external achievements (money, awards, social status).
- Often comes with pressure to prove yourself to others.
- Can lead to stress, competition, and never feeling like it's enough.

Golden Rule: Success without meaning feels empty in the long run.

Chasing Meaning

- Focuses on internal fulfillment and making a difference.
- Brings happiness from within, not just from external rewards.

- Leads to a life where success is a byproduct of purpose.

Golden Rule: When you chase meaning, success often follows naturally.

What Happens When You Only Chase Success?

1. Many people who achieve great success still feel unhappy and unfulfilled.
2. A rich businessman may have everything but no true happiness.
3. A famous celebrity may have millions of fans but still feel lonely.
4. A top student may get perfect grades but feel lost about their future.

Golden Rule: Success alone doesn't guarantee happiness—meaning does.

How to Chase Meaning Instead of Just Success

1. Define What Truly Matters to You

- Ask yourself:
- What makes me feel alive?
- What kind of impact do I want to make?
- What would I do even if I wasn't paid for it?

Golden Rule: True success is when you live in alignment with your values.

2. Focus on Growth, Not Just Achievement

- Instead of only chasing grades, awards, or money, focus on:
- Becoming the best version of yourself.
- Learning new skills that help you grow.
- Building relationships and experiences that bring joy.

Golden Rule: Personal growth is the real definition of success.

3. Choose Purpose Over Popularity

- Don't just do what's trendy—do what feels right.
- Make decisions based on your values, not social pressure.
- Understand that real fulfillment comes from meaning, not just success.

Golden Rule: Chasing popularity leads to temporary highs—chasing meaning leads to lasting happiness.

4. Use Success as a Tool, Not the Goal

- Success should serve your purpose, not replace it.
- Money, fame, or influence can be used to create impact—but they shouldn't define your worth.
- Work hard, but never lose sight of why you're doing it.

Golden Rule: Let success be a result of your meaningful work, not your only aim.

Success Without Meaning is Empty

Chasing success without purpose is like running in a race with no finish line—it never feels like enough.

But when you chase meaning, success becomes a natural outcome, not an endless struggle.

So ask yourself today: Do I want to just be successful, or do I want to live a life of meaning?

Because a meaningful life is the greatest success of all.

With belief in you,
AG

CHAPTER XXXVII

What I Wish I Knew When I Was Your Age

Dear Teenager,

If I could go back in time and talk to my younger self, there are so many things I would say. Life has taught me lessons that I wish I had known earlier—lessons that would have saved me from stress, doubt, and wasted time.

Since I can't go back, I'm sharing them with you **so that you don't have to learn them the hard way.**

1. Your Grades Matter, But They Don't Define You

- Do your best in school, but don't believe that your worth is based on marks.
- Some of the most successful people weren't top students—they were just lifelong learners.
- Focus on understanding concepts, developing skills, and being curious.

Golden Rule: Your education is important, but your self-worth is not measured by a report card.

2. People's Opinions Don't Matter as Much as You Think

- Stop worrying about what others think of you—most of them are too busy worrying about themselves.
- No matter what you do, some people will judge. Do it anyway.
- The only opinion that truly matters is yours.

Golden Rule: You don't need everyone's approval—just your own confidence.

3. Build Skills, Not Just Resumes

- The world rewards real skills—communication, problem-solving, leadership, and creativity.
- School won't teach you everything—learn on your own.
- Find hobbies, take online courses, read books, and explore things that excite you.

Golden Rule: Skills will take you further than any degree ever will.

4. Failures Are Not the End—They Are the Beginning

- You will make mistakes. You will fail at something. And that's okay.
- Every failure teaches you something valuable—learn from it instead of fearing it.
- The most successful people failed more than others ever tried.

Golden Rule: Fail fast, learn faster, and never stop moving

forward.

5. The Friends You Choose Will Shape Your Future

- Surround yourself with positive, ambitious, and kind people.
- A bad friend can ruin your mindset and hold you back from growth.
- Quality matters more than quantity—it's better to have a few real friends than a hundred fake ones.

Golden Rule: Your circle determines your success—choose wisely.

6. Social Media is a Trap If You Let It Be

- It's not real life—people only show the highlights, not their struggles.
- Too much scrolling can make you feel like you're "not enough."
- Use social media as a tool for learning and growth, not just for comparison.

Golden Rule: Create more than you consume—build something meaningful instead of just watching others.

7. Money Habits You Build Now Will Shape Your Future

- Learn about saving, investing, and managing money early.

- Avoid debt, control your spending, and understand that financial freedom gives you choices.
- Money itself won't make you happy, but being financially smart will give you security and peace.

Golden Rule: Control your money, or your money will control you.

8. Confidence Comes From Action, Not Waiting

- Stop waiting until you "feel ready" to do something—start before you're ready.
- Confidence grows when you take action, not from overthinking.
- Speak up, try new things, and trust yourself.

Golden Rule: The more you step out of your comfort zone, the stronger you become.

9. Don't Chase Success—Chase Meaning

- Success is great, but a meaningful life is greater.
- Find work that excites you, makes a difference, and aligns with who you are.
- Success is not just about money—it's about growth, impact, and happiness.

Golden Rule: A fulfilled life is one where you wake up excited, not just rich.

10. Time is the Most Valuable Thing You Have—Use it Wisely

- You won't realize how fast time goes until it's gone—don't waste it on distractions.
- Invest in yourself—learn, grow, and build something meaningful.
- The small choices you make daily shape your future.

Golden Rule: Spend your time creating a future you'll be proud of.

You Have So Much Potential—Don't Waste It

There is so much ahead of you—so many opportunities, experiences, and lessons waiting for you.

So take risks, work hard, be kind, and never stop learning.

Because your future is in your hands, and you have the power to make it amazing.

With belief in you,
AG

A Final Letter: The Future Is Yours

Dear Teenager,

As you turn the last page of this book, I want you to pause for a moment and think about this:

Your future is a blank page, and you hold the pen.

Everything you dream of, everything you hope to achieve—it's all within your reach. **But only if you choose to take action.**

The Truth About Life

Life is not always fair. It will challenge you, test you, and push you in ways you never expected. But in those moments, **you will grow, you will learn, and you will rise.**

There will be failures, but they will teach you resilience.
There will be doubts, but they will make you stronger.
There will be tough choices, but they will shape who you become.

You Are Capable of More Than You Think

You have potential beyond what you see today.
You have the ability to **change your own life and impact the world around you.**
You have the power to write your own story—not one written by fear, but by courage and purpose.

What I Hope You Take Away From This Book

1. Believe in yourself, even when others don't.
2. Work hard, but work smart—focus on what truly matters.
3. Surround yourself with the right people—they will shape your future.
4. Never stop learning, growing, and improving yourself.
5. Make choices that align with your values, not just what's popular.
6. Help others along the way—your kindness will always come back to you.

The Future Belongs to Those Who Create It

No one is going to hand you success. No one is going to live your dreams for you. It's up to you.

You can spend your life waiting for the "right time" or the "perfect opportunity," or you can start now—learning, building, growing, and becoming the person you were meant to be.

Your future is not determined by your background, your past mistakes, or what others think of you. It is determined by the choices you make today.

So, my final advice to you is this:

1. Dream big, but take action.
2. Work hard, but enjoy the journey.
3. Be fearless in the face of challenges.
4. Live a life of meaning, not just success.
5. And never, ever give up on yourself.

Because the **future is yours. And it's waiting for you to make it extraordinary.**

With belief in you,
AG

Your Action Plan For A Great Life

Dear Teenager,

Reading this book is a great start—but **real change happens when you take action.** Knowledge is powerful, but only when you use it.

Here's **your action plan** to apply everything you've learned and build a life you're proud of.

Step 1: Define Your Vision for Life

What kind of person do you want to become?
What are your biggest dreams and goals?
What kind of impact do you want to make?

ACTION: Write down your vision for the next 5 years. Don't just think about success—think about meaning, growth, and contribution.

Step 2: Develop the Right Mindset

Success starts in your mind. You need to train it to think in a way that empowers you.

Believe in yourself—even when others don't.
Focus on **growth over perfection**—keep learning.
See failures as lessons, not roadblocks.

ACTION: Start a "Growth Journal." Every day, write one thing you learned, one challenge you overcame, and one small success.

Step 3: Master Your Time & Habits

Your time is your most valuable asset—use it wisely.

Stop wasting time on distractions that don't add value.
Set daily, weekly, and monthly goals.
Build strong habits—what you do every day determines your future.

ACTION: Make a morning routine that sets the tone for success (exercise, reading, planning your day). Stick to it.

Step 4: Focus on Skills, Not Just Degrees

Your future depends on what you can do, not just what you know.

Improve your communication, leadership, and problem-solving skills.
Learn financial literacy—how to save, invest, and grow wealth.
Take online courses, read books, and never stop learning.

ACTION: Choose one high-value skill to master in the next year (public speaking, writing, coding, business, etc.).

Step 5: Surround Yourself with the Right People

Your environment shapes your future.

Spend time with people who inspire and challenge you.

Distance yourself from negativity and toxic influences.
Find mentors—people who have achieved what you want.

ACTION: Make a list of 5 people who uplift you. Make a plan to learn from them, spend time with them, or follow their work.

Step 6: Take Care of Your Health (Physical & Mental)

Your body and mind are your greatest assets. Take care of them.

Exercise daily—movement fuels energy and confidence.
Eat healthy—good food fuels a good life.
Take care of your mental health—manage stress, avoid burnout, and practice mindfulness.

ACTION: Set a fitness goal for the next 3 months (work out 3-5 times a week, eat less junk food, get better sleep).

Step 7: Give More Than You Take

True fulfillment comes from making a difference.

Help someone every day—even small acts count.
Give without expecting anything in return.
Use your skills, time, or resources to make the world better.

ACTION: Choose one way to give back (volunteering, mentoring, helping a friend, supporting a cause).

Step 8: Take Bold Action Every Day

Thinking and planning are great, but action is what changes your life.

Stop overthinking and start doing.
Take risks—growth happens outside your comfort zone.
Be consistent—even small daily actions lead to huge results.

ACTION: Write down one bold action you will take TODAY toward your dream—then go do it.

Your Life is in Your Hands

- No one else is going to build your dream life for you—it's up to you to take action.
- If you follow this plan, stay disciplined, and never stop growing, your future will be extraordinary.

Start today. Start small. But most importantly, start NOW.

Because the best time to change your life is this very moment.

With belief in you,
AG